Evangelism Memories and Streets of Gold

~~

Charlotte Brown Garrick

www.TEACHServices.com • (800) 367-1844

World rights reserved. This book or any portion thereof may not be copied or reproduced in any form or manner whatever, except as provided by law, without the written permission of the publisher, except by a reviewer who may quote brief passages in a review.

The author assumes full responsibility for the accuracy and interpretation of the Ellen White quotations cited in this book. Unless otherwise indicated, all scripture quotations are taken from the King James Version of the Bible.

Copyright © 2021 **Charlotte Brown Garrick**

Copyright © 2021 TEACH Services, Inc.

ISBN-13: 978-1-4796-1222-2 (Paperback)

ISBN-13: 978-1-4796-1223-9 (ePub)

Library of Congress Control Number: 2020920229

All scripture quotations, unless otherwise indicated, are taken from the King James Version. Public domain.

Table of Contents

FOREWORD 7
CHAPTER ONE 9
    Beginnings 9
    The Special Guests 10
    Who Are You, God? 10
    The Books 11
    Who Are These People? 11
    An Awakening 12
    Family Evangelism? 13
    Becoming Adventist 15
    Ingathering 17
    Are You a Vegetarian? 17
    A Time of Decisions 19
CHAPTER TWO 20
    The Beautiful Place 20
    The Crusade 20
    New Commitments for Jesus 21
CHAPTER THREE 23
    On the Road 23
    Minnesota 23
    The Board of Education? 24
    George's Debut 24
    Finding His Path 25
    Florida 26
    New Sabbath Keepers 26
    What Did You Say? 26

Fun for All 27
Meaning Well 28
Tornado Country 28
Seeking the Lost 28
A Turn in the Road 29

CHAPTER FOUR 31
Ashe County 31
Living Room Evangelism 31
Bluegrass Musicians for the Lord 32
The Running Preacher Man 34
A Hell-Fire Sermon 34
An Asbestos Body? 34
The Light Shines Brightly in a "Dark County" 35
Wading out into Deep Waters 36
Life and Near-Death Experiences 36
Tried as by Fire 37
An Angel? 38
The Bright Light 39
We Are Loved No Matter What 42
"When It Rains, It Pours" 43

CHAPTER FIVE 45
Overseas and Back 45
Onward and Upward 45
The Awesome Invitation 46
The Ghilenskis 46
Opening Night in Kishinev, Moldova 47
Bibles and Baptisms 49
The Villages 51
A Moldovan Historic Event 52
Farewell! 54
The Big White Truck 55

CHAPTER SIX—Stateside Again! 57
All Around Florida with the Brownlows 57
Going Around and Around in a Field 57

A Typical Crusade	58
All Hands on Deck	59
Follow Me, Please!	59
Elmer and Mabel	61
Miami Beach and Halloween in South Florida	62
Cats!	62
A Demon in the House	64
Keep on Keeping On	64
The Horse Story	65
A 3ABN Encounter	66

CHAPTER SEVEN 68
    This and That 68
    In Appreciation 69
    Humanity in Action 69
    Chicken? 70
    Punch, Anyone? 71
    First Impressions? 71
    George in a Tuxedo? 72
    Going to a Lot of Trouble 73
    Is It a Secret? 74
    Come, Lord Jesus! 74

CHAPTER EIGHT 75
    New Paths 75
    Winds over Opryland and Beyond 77
    Vocal Cords Repaired Here 78
    The Contract! 79
    Cats? 80
    A Secret Revealed! 81
    The Unexpected Conversion 83

CHAPTER NINE 84
    Trails West 84
    Wachula 84
    Haines City 85
    "Soup, Anyone?" 86

Sky Writing?	87
Bernie Pounds	87
Razor Wire	87
Hindrances?	89
A Hurting Heart!	90
Breaking North Carolina Ties	91
An Unwanted Guest!!	91
Intruders	92
CHAPTER TEN	**93**
To the Mountain and Back	93
St. Johns, Arizona	94
Unwanted!	95
The Fire	96
A Change of Direction	96
San Bernardino, California	96
A Life Taken	97
CHAPTER ELEVEN	**101**
What About Wickenburg?	101
Burger King?	103
The Man in the Dream	103
You've Found It!	104
The Halvorsens Again!	106
The Piano	106
Strong Shoulders	108
CHAPTER TWELVE	**109**
The List	109
EPILOGUE	**113**

Foreword

As an avid reader I enjoy all types of books, but the two types of books I love the most are biographies and story books. The book you hold in your hands is both. The story of Charlotte and George Garrick is a remarkable story of God's grace and divine movement in their lives, as well as countless stories of the amazing miracles they witness together on life's journey as servants of Christ.

This book is like a combination of the fast-paced gospel of Mark, with the powerful and exciting stories of Erik B. Hare. The only difference is that George and Charlotte are not "retelling" stories they've heard from others—they are telling stories from their own personal experiences.

It has been a privilege for my wife, Lillian, and I to have known the Garricks for nearly two decades, and as I read this volume I was touched with stories that even I had never had a chance to hear. It is heart-warming and uplifting to read how God has worked in the lives of these two very special people. I'm so thankful to be able to call George and Charlotte my friends.

I believe you will be touched and inspired as well with the way God has worked with this amazing, dedicated, truly Christian couple.

—Ed Keyes, Arizona Conference President

Chapter One

Beginnings

Evangelism! A word cherished and full of meaning when one considers that Jesus was our Great Evangelist when He came to live among us to show us the way home. It has been said that evangelism is the very heart of Christianity, and it is. Especially is this so in light of our time in history. This is so true in the daily news of fulfillment of some verses in Matthew 24. Jesus sends each and every one of us to evangelize in his or her own way. Some are preachers, some teachers, some housewives, and the list goes on and on.

I was an ordinary person who wanted to be involved, and the following account is, at first, mostly the revelation of my own personal journey toward heaven down the path of evangelism; though, later in the story I will include much of my husband George's own experiences with mine. You'll see how God led us into Adventism and how our lives were joined in one grand purpose along the evangelism trail. You will experience interesting "behind-the-scenes" moments. This account has been prepared and presented in an informal and conversational style to enhance the stories and to preserve them, and this will reveal how God can use imperfect people to work out His perfect will.

When I think back over our lives, I realize how very gracious and kind God was to us in allowing our childhood dreams of evangelism to come true. It was more than we could have hoped for in the beginning; however, it was not to become a reality until we became young adults. Even so, it was in God's own timing.

I grew up as a member of the Pentecostal Holiness Church. My childhood was a time of preparation with church attendance and in Bible study, involvement in choirs, trios, piano lessons, and, on many occasions, playing for church. School days were filled with music in plays and choral groups. I'm thankful for teachers who gave their students opportunities to express inclinations toward music and art. Those were the formative years when ideals were birthed and tucked away into a deep place in my inner being to be set free for the Lord years later. I didn't realize that at that time.

My father passed away when I was a young girl of seventeen, therefore, I had to put on hold dreams and plans and begin to make my way through the world for daily sustenance. My father was only forty-four when he died of a massive heart attack, and that forever changed our lives as a family. Nothing was ever the same again, and to this day I find myself still grieving on each anniversary of his death.

My mother was a devout Christian, and she encouraged us as children to follow Jesus as our Savior. Usually Mom sat by her favorite window each afternoon to study the Scriptures. And church was the first destination for each of her six children as they became part of the family. It didn't matter that we didn't own a car. Dad and Mom lit the lantern, and we walked through the woods at night to church if there was a revival in progress. Mom taught us that the Bible, including both the Old and New Testaments, is a living record of God's presence to us.

The Special Guests

Another influence in my early years was the fact that every evangelist who ever came to do a revival at our church stayed at our house. It was known around town that Mama was an excellent cook, and we lived in a huge two-story house that provided a guest room for the preacher—even if it became the lot for one of us children to sleep on a quilt. Motels were not available then as they are these days. We children had to be quiet during the day because "the preacher was resting and studying for the sermon to be presented that night at church." This meant that we attended each and every night! We learned to talk and act respectfully around these men and women of God. Mama insisted that we were on our best behavior, and this was such good training for the future role that I would play.

Who Are You, God?

I distinctly remember the spring day that I began wondering about the existence of God. I was sitting on our back porch where the washing machine was rumbling on as it cleaned our clothes. As I sat there, I remember the questions that began to surface in my innermost thoughts and how the answers must somehow influence me in what I should become in my life. It seemed almost too profound for one so young as I, but the questions were there, and God knew that I needed answers. I can't remember the exact date, but I did know that I needed a Savior, and I gave my heart to Jesus who died on the cross for my pardon. The Holy Spirit spoke to my young heart, and He is still speaking to those who will heed His call.

The Books

One hot, muggy, summer day when I was probably ten, two gentlemen came to our door. (And I know that they were accompanied by angels. Looking back, I think it must have been Elders Blake and I. W. Young.) They were selling Christian literature, and this was of great interest to my mother. She invited them into the living room where they showed her the Christian books that they were making available for her to purchase. Mom liked *Bible Readings for the Home* and *The Marked Bible* and ordered them.

When these books were delivered, I don't think any of us, at first, read them. Perhaps Mom thumbed through them. They were simply put into the bookcase to be pulled out by my young hands a little later when I became a teenager. When I discovered these books, I read them off and on, but with limited understanding of their true meaning for me. The leaders of my Pentecostal Holiness Church asked me to serve as program director for our young people's meetings. This meant that I needed material for my programs; I turned to *Bible Readings for the Home* for ideas.

After several times of presenting this material, I was gently reprimanded by the song leader to stop using this book for my programs, but I was too far gone. The pictures and significant information were stored in my young mind. There was one illustration showing the Sabbath going all the way back to creation, and that would come back to my recall as you will see. I pondered over the passage in Exodus 20, and especially verses 8–11, but I don't remember ever hearing any sermon on that section of the Bible. It was significant, however, that we were taught and believed a literal week of creation. I've always been thankful for that. I wondered and wondered about the Sabbath, but I didn't know how to act upon this knowledge until my early adulthood when I left home to seek employment after my father's death.

Who Are These People?

Another incident that happened in my young life was during a family drive through the city of Winston-Salem, North Carolina. As we passed this one church on Patterson Avenue, I noticed a man out in front working on the church grounds. It was on Sunday, and I asked my mother why someone would be working on Sunday as this man was doing. She answered me, "Those people are known as Seventh-day Adventists. They go to church on Saturday." I put that statement into my memory bank for later.

Throughout my childhood I was always adding to that memory bank and was known as "Question Box." Everything was a question for me, and it still is. One of my intense questions to my mother was: "Look at the calendar, Mama. Sunday is the first day of the week. Why do we keep that instead of the seventh day?"

She answered me without skipping a beat, "We keep Sunday because of tradition." (Looking back to that time, I believe Mom got her answer from secretly reading *Bible Readings for the Home*.) That we keep Sunday because of tradition was all that she said, and I didn't ask anything more. Then later, when I began my search as an adult, I vividly remembered her words. How well she had taught me, and she wasn't even aware of it! Surely the Lord directed her words to me for future times. I will always be amazed at this considering the turn of events in my life.

> *That we keep Sunday because of tradition was all that she said, and I didn't ask anything more. Then later, when I began my search as an adult, I vividly remembered her words*

An Awakening

Shortly before my father passed away, he gave me the privilege of taking his place in a pilgrimage to an Oral Roberts tent meeting in Norfolk, Virginia. In my young mind, and in that time and place, I thought Oral Roberts was a powerful and dynamic speaker, but for me, he was not the only star that day. I was completely in awe of the lady on stage responsible for the musical background for the meetings.

Hundreds of people were all around me, but I was oblivious to them. I was intently watching the blonde-haired lady at the organ whose music tied all the elements of the service into one grand moment in time. In fact, I watched her all during the service. I was hooked. To me this was the seed of evangelism placed into my young heart. Yes, I was hooked, as they say, and I knew that I would enjoy being in that role as part of evangelistic efforts. The music spoke to me, and I knew what I really wanted to do and be when the time came for me to emerge in adulthood. I made sure that I attended these meetings at every opportunity from then on, mostly because of the lady on stage.

Recently I met the niece of that very same lady, who by this time was in her eighties. The niece said that she would tell her aunt that she inspired a young girl so long ago. Unknown to me at the time was the fact that this lady was a Seventh-day Adventist Christian, and she was the musician for the Oral Roberts crusades. I was amazed at that revelation.

In the city where I was employed after I left my childhood home, I met some Adventist people through a work acquaintance, and I was immediately intrigued by what I was hearing from them. Old questions began to arise, and I knew that I could finally find answers. I began to study Adventist books, took the Voice of Prophecy Bible lessons, attended Elder Cemer's evangelistic meetings, and I was subsequently baptized.

Apparently, a church designer in those days had gone through the South designing baptistries that were hidden in the floor of each church's rostrum. I had never seen anything like that. When I was a young girl I was baptized in a creek, but I chose to be baptized again since I had learned new truths from God's Word. But I'll never forget the experience of seeing the deacons of my new church lift up a section of the platform where a baptismal pool awaited my descent into it. It was totally different, but I accepted the situation, spider webs and all, and I was very happy in the Lord. I was a new Sabbath keeper, and I was joyful in my new experience. That was in 1952.

Family Evangelism?

When I went back home to tell my mother about my new-found faith, from all appearances she almost had a heart attack. I went over to her bookcase, took out *Bible Readings for the Home,* and showed her that picture of the Sabbath going back to creation. She then grabbed the book from my hands and began tearing pages out one by one and dropping them in a heap at my feet. I was devastated, but what could I say? I probably wept. I don't remember much about anything else that was said because of the circumstances. She was my mother, and I had wounded her deeply by departing from the church that she dearly loved. But I had to follow the Bible. In my studies I had learned how the Roman Catholic Church claimed to have the authority to change the day of worship from the seventh day, Saturday, to the first day, Sunday. I tried to tell her new things; however, she was not in a receptive mode, and I soon left to go back to my place.

Mom wasn't the only one to come against me in my new choices in my spiritual journey. My oldest brother, Garvey, decided that he would add his two cents' worth in connection to my choices in our health message. I remember the time when I was sitting on the front porch of our home place, that as he walked by my chair, he sarcastically said, "Charlotte, you know that you want some of that good ole ham." I chose to ignore that statement because I was firm in my new knowledge of the harmful effects of eating pork.

(Years later, Garvey and his wife, Helen, became camping buddies, and they were lots of fun to be with. We tried not to impose any doctrinal views their way; however, sometimes a word or conversation would head that way, and we would have to answer with truth. In one instance, the subject of the right church suddenly appeared, and we gave answers according to scripture. Garvey replied that he had "his way" all mapped out. To that Helen said very emphatically, "Yes, and if he goes to hell, I'm going with him!" On our part, those words produced shock, dismay, and sadness to think that she would go that far in her loyalty to him. We all stand individually before God to answer alone for ourselves and for our choices. Garvey and Helen simply closed their minds to any further information about that subject and the other truths that he rejected.)

Then there was my sister, Ruth, whom I adored when I was a child being carried around on her little hip. She, who had been my first piano teacher, disappointed me when I tried to tell her about my wonderful news regarding the Sabbath and all the other great things that are shown to us from God's Word. She didn't attack any particular doctrine; she just told me that she had made up her mind on the subject of religion, and she didn't want to hear anything that I had to say about my new walk with God.

(An interesting thing happened years later when we all were much, much older. George and I treated Ruth and her husband to a meal in a famous restaurant in Tennessee. This place was known for its barbecue of both beef and pork and other menu items—she chose a pork meal. At that time, I felt that her choice of pork was in defiance of what I stood for in the way of diet. Unbeknownst to me, she told me later that she became "as sick as a dog" in the aftermath of eating that choice of food.)

On that note, there was another time in our waning years that I remarked to her, "Ruth, my religion has been an offense to you, hasn't it?" To that she just nodded her head in agreement. I went on to say, "It's been lonely all these years to have been the only one in my family who embraced this message."

She almost hung her head as she answered me very softly, "Honey, I'll bet it has." For a fleeting second it almost sounded like King Agrippa who seemed to have come near to accepting Paul's persuasion in Acts 26:27, 28. "King Agrippa, believest thou the prophets? I know that thou believest.. Then Agrippa said unto Paul, Almost thou persuades me to be a Christian." So close, and yet so far away. How does one end a conversation like that with my sister? I decided to give her completely to the Lord.

Now, something that really brought a sting to my heart was the experience of losing these two elderly brothers back in 2015. The brother next to me, Morris, always resisted any attempt on my part to tell him about more knowledge available to him from the Bible. It was conflict every time that subject was mentioned. At the last, I went into his nursing home room and started to ask about his spiritual wellbeing with no thought of presenting any doctrine. I was stopped short with his statement, "Charlotte, don't start that stuff." And he was at that point near death. (He passed away soon after that visit.)

To my readers: What I've just revealed in telling these instances is the fact that when one learns of new truths and makes the choice to follow them, then it is certain that resistance will come from family, friends, and the clergy. Count on this possibly happening, and I will say that family evangelism is difficult at times.

Even Jesus made the statement in Matthew 13:57, 58. "And they were offended in him. But Jesus said unto them, A prophet is not without honor, save in his own country, and in his own house. And he did not many mighty works there because of their unbelief." That is the principle of what I've told you about in my own family. To be able to endure this rejection one must pray lots, hold on to God's hand, and read and study the Bible. It hurts when it happens to one's enthusiasm, but just keep on loving them in spite of all that they say.

Becoming Adventist

To leave my friends with whom I had grown up was a hard thing to do. We had played together; we had gone to school and church together; and we had even double-dated together. These young people were, essentially, family to me. After I became an Adventist, these friends were still sweet and kind to me, but an invisible wall of separation had now come between us, and I had to move on with my new life.

I will say to my readers that when new people make a decision to follow the Lord in baptism and become a member of the Seventh-day Adventist Church, they are making multiple decisions at that time. They leave a familiar worship style and place; they leave family; they leave friends, and they mostly leave old lifestyles. I remember the stress I felt when I first did my ironing on Sunday. I knew that it was the first day of the week, but still it was customary for me not to work on that day—I had to start a new way of thinking regarding that.

While all these changes are being resolved, new converts are in a mode of learning and processing new truths from the Bible. It is very important for new people to form new friendships immediately after baptism. I strongly recommend that concept. I was thereafter blessed to be included immediately into a friendship with several young people who loved and followed the Lord. A firm support group is needed for encouragement in a new setting. I recently heard an Adventist television minster refer to these relationships as similar to the old custom of sitting on the "front porch" and conversing with neighbors and friends.

Along the lines of this particular subject of new people and their assimilation into the Adventist church, I want to take this a step further to reveal where I was when I joined the church. Fortunately, I was already a student of the Bible and therefore knew the books of the Bible. But at first, I was totally confused by the "lingo" that was used each week at church and in casual conversation with other members. What in the world do they mean by "Harvest Ingathering?" Then there was: *"Listen, These Times, Review*, Wham, Choplets, Missionary Volunteers, Minute Man, Happy Sabbath, The Truth, Lay Activities, Week of Prayer, The Blessed Hope," and others. Also, the tithe envelope was a mystery until it was explained to me. I had wondered if I was expected to give to each line presented on the envelope.

I had a lot of learning to do, and so do all the other new people who become one of us. Let's take the time to explain these common everyday terms that are so familiar to us as Adventists. By the way, when I first became an Adventist a friend brought me a can of gluten chops to cook so that I could be Adventist in my cooking. I was dumbfounded as to what I should do with the contents, and looking back, I think it was a disaster. And the incident didn't contribute much toward my religious experience.

Ingathering

Speaking of ingathering, we used methods in the early years that aren't used anymore—I hope. I remember the first time that I was handed the blue can, and a few dollar bills were placed so that they were sticking out at the top of the can. Have you ever gone ingathering in front of a liquor store? I have. That is where they took two of us young women so that we could use our feminine charms to induce the patrons to place money into our cans. My girlfriend used to take their hand that was full of change from inside the store and pour it all into her can. Then she would laugh.

One night I was standing in front of this particular liquor store, and I saw a car go by with a former boyfriend, Randall, from my previous church, sitting at the wheel. I saw him stare at me in disbelief. I had no way of telling him about my purpose in being there, and I'm sure that he thought that I had backslidden and had taken up the liquor habit. He probably thought that I was waiting for a friend to come back out with "our" purchase.

I heard many stories about ingathering, however, none was so vivid as the one where one of our young men went into a dance hall and got permission to solicit money by going in and out among the dancers. That would not be permitted these days. Perhaps we could call that "The Ingathering Waltz." I did accompany our pastor to many business places during the day, and we received some nice gifts. That seemed to me to be the best way over the options of the liquor store, dance hall, or other questionable places.

This same ingathering girlfriend from the liquor store once went to a nearby small town and went into a pool hall to ingather. One of the church men went in before her and took a seat. When she came in, he put money into her can, thus, he became an example for the other men to follow. The only thing that the two of them didn't count on was that the entire group of men followed her out onto the sidewalk, making some unwanted remarks to her. My friend said that was a scary situation for a few moments. I didn't think that method was so good either, and I never went into a pool hall or directly into a liquor store to ingather.

Are You a Vegetarian?

After I became an Adventist, I became convinced that I should become a vegetarian. I remembered hog-killing time as we were growing up, and it was a terrible thing in so many ways. I know that when the men arrived to help my daddy with this slaughtering, I would run upstairs and hide my head under my pillow to lessen the sound of the gun used for this purpose. Before the helpers arrived, Daddy had built a framework high in the air with the capability of jerking the hogs up by their hind feet after they were shot in the head. Their throats were slit, and soon after that the process of salting down the meat began for preservation.

I used to watch that part of it with repugnance. I know that there were washtubs placed around the yard to hold the different parts of the hogs. There were the hams, the shoulders, the internal organs, and yes, the intestines, to put it bluntly. These were cleaned and then placed in the oven to be "rendered out" for the chitterlings. I'm thankful that I never ate any of the inside parts, but I am more thankful for the knowledge of the harmful effects of pork eating.

> *I made the decision to become a vegetarian. Later I told my mother about this, and to this announcement she replied, "Honey, Jesus ate meat."*

When I was about thirteen, Mom was having trouble with her stomach, and our doctor advised her to stay away from pork. Soon after that, Daddy came inside one day and announced to Mom that he didn't think that he would raise hogs anymore. He said he thought that they were unclean. So it wasn't hard for me to become a vegetarian with Daddy doing this background training for me. One other notable thing about the hog killing: Each year at that time, it seemed that almost everyone in our family would become sick after eating the first tenderloin of the "kill," so to speak.

I made the decision to become a vegetarian. Later I told my mother about this, and to this announcement she replied, "Honey, Jesus ate meat." I hardly had an answer for that, but I did try to tell her the benefits of being vegetarian. Adam and Eve ate the perfect diet, and I wanted to try to come as close to that as I could considering the fact that we are so far from those times and circumstances. But I wanted to try. By this time, Mom's love for me had outweighed her protests against my religious feelings, and she was more receptive to a point.

A Time of Decisions

For some reason, my parents never told my brothers, sisters, and me that they loved us. Perhaps it was because they were never told by their parents that they were loved. Therefore, during this time of breaking home ties with my mother, she startled me by saying, "You know that you are the 'apple of my eye,' don't you?" Once she humbly asked me to go to a Christian college in Franklin Springs, Georgia. She said if I would go, she would take out her savings and fund my education there. Since she was a widow, I knew that her savings were very meager. I knew that would be a great sacrifice for her, but it meant that she was showing her love for me. I realized that she was trying one more thing to change my mind about my becoming an Adventist. I never had any plans for an education at that institution, so her suggestion was silently rejected.

In her older years she became loyal to me and to my faith. She told me about a mission report at her church, and that she had spoken up and told them that the Adventists led the world in missions—she was "sticking up for me" in her own way. At the end of her life when I would sometimes visit her on Sabbath afternoon, I noticed that everything was done, and that she was just resting. We believed that she was in an ostensible way trying to keep both days "just in case." Certainly, I won't be her Judge. God will. I have her to thank for instilling in me a love and respect for the Bible and spiritual matters and inadvertently paving the way for me to become a Seventh-day Adventist Christian.

Another note about the books that Mom bought from those salesmen so long ago: It was interesting in my college years that I, too, sold these religious books. I, too, was known as a colporteur. Praise the Lord! As for the *Bible Readings for the Home* that Mom ripped apart and dropped at my feet, I found another one just like that one that was destroyed. I felt that something had come full circle.

Chapter Two

The Beautiful Place

To move ahead in the story I will of necessity leave out many details of personal, day-to-day living. My early marriage had ended, but I was blessed with two wonderful, caring, and beautiful daughters from that interval in my life. There is always a lot of hurt and regret as the result of an ending. I was at that time living in Western North Carolina where the girls were attending school. I later married George Garrick, Jr.

The Crusade

George's background was very similar to mine as to place of childhood in Salisbury, in the Piedmont section of North Carolina. The difference was the fact that he came from a staunch Baptist heritage. George Garrick, Sr. believed that if a revival was happening in a radius of ten miles, then they as a family should attend and support this meeting. It didn't matter the denomination. They went. Many times he volunteered George, Jr. and his sisters to go up front and sing, something that they as children disliked very much, however, they obeyed their father's wishes for them.

One night they were on their way to a meeting somewhere in town, and over the street was a banner advertising a crusade in a nearby auditorium. George, Jr. asked his dad if he would like to go there instead of to the previous place. Plans were changed, and the crusade was where they went that night. Elder Cemer again happened to be the one doing a presentation on the Sabbath.

George, Sr. was so impressed with this new truth that he asked George, Jr. if he would go to their Baptist church and talk with the pastor about the Sabbath. Then he added that George, Jr. should also go to the Catholic Church where he mowed grass and ask the "Father" there about the change of the Sabbath.

George, Jr. first went to their pastor and asked him about the change. This man was very honest with George and admitted that Saturday was the biblical Sabbath. Then George, Jr. went to the local Catholic Church and asked the priest there what day was the Sabbath. He truthfully told him that the Roman Catholic Church did indeed change that day. (They thought to change it.) George asked him which was the correct church to belong to if one wanted to attend one that went completely by the Bible. This older priest told him to go down Main Street and turn left on Chestnut Street and on the right would be a Seventh-day Adventist Church. He said that was where he should go if he wanted to go strictly by the Bible. He further stated that of all Protestant churches, the Adventist church was the nearest to the Bible of any.

That clinched it for the Garrick family, and they subsequently studied further truths from the Bible. As a family, they were eventually baptized into the Seventh-day Adventist Church. George is a graduate of Mount Pisgah Academy in Western North Carolina, and he attended colleges at Collegedale and Cleveland, Tennessee. He finished his college work with a combined status of Registered X-ray and Laboratory Technologist. George has two beautiful, sweet daughters from a previous marriage.

New Commitments for Jesus

When George and I were married we had both wandered away from the Lord and from the Church. We were hurting, and in time, like two lost lambs, Jesus found us and carried us in His arms back to the fold. We returned to the Lord and made new commitments to Him. We became involved in working in our chosen Adventist church—George with "sound" and electronics, and I was interested in helping with the music. George is good at doing whatever he tries to do: his profession, carpentry, electrical, plumbing, and yes, even cooking. Our new commitments to the Lord led to our wanting to help out, if needed, in other churches in the area.

We both had come back to the Lord with the sole purpose of doing whatever He wanted us to do. We have found over the years that if we make ourselves available to the Lord, He will make a way for us to be used by Him. At that time, we still had the daughters to guide through their schooling, but we found time for spiritual things.

It was at this point that our neighbors, the former General Conference President of Seventh-day Adventists, Elder Robert Pierson, and a local pastor, Elder Percy Manuel, came to our house and invited us to help with a new work in the area. (Both ministers are now deceased.) We responded eagerly, and we thoroughly enjoyed doing what we were asked to do. Other areas began to open up for us to extend our expertise in "helping out." I was beginning to get the feel of evangelism on a local level, however, God had plans for us that we couldn't yet know about.

Our congregation was in the process of building, and George was asked to plan a fundraising event. George is one of the most tenacious and enthusiastic individuals that I have ever known, and when he is asked to do something, he does it with all his strength and might. (This would prove to be a great asset for him in later years when he would become an evangelist and pastor.) For the fund raising he asked two local musicians and me to join with him in a community-wide "singspiration" to do an appeal for offerings toward our building project. We sang, played instruments, and had audience participation in hymn singing. At that time, an offering of fifteen hundred dollars was considered a great success, and besides, everyone had fun during the event.

It was during this most happy time in a wondrously beautiful setting that I was invited to sing for Elder and Mrs. Robert Pierson's "Golden Wedding Anniversary" celebration. I'll never forget singing "Let Me Call You Sweetheart" for this outstanding couple on this very special occasion. They were so sweet and kind to George and me. We felt so unworthy of such love; however, we were grateful for the opportunity to be a part of this moment. I still have the cassette tapes of classical music which were presented to me in appreciation of my musical contribution to their special celebration. In future years, George was interim pastor where some of their relatives lived. We never know where the Lord will lead us.

Chapter Three

On the Road

In the fall of 1982, evangelist Bill Waters and his wife, Cora "Sunshine," came to our area in Hendersonville, North Carolina, for an evangelistic crusade. George found great joy in helping backstage with the sound and computer equipment for the many projectors needed in their multimedia presentations. As I said about my early exposure to crusades, we were hooked on evangelism. Subsequently, Bill and Sunshine invited us to go on the road with them for at least ten other evangelistic campaigns. We were on our way on an adventure for God that has never stopped. I hope it continues until Jesus comes again.

In 1983, George was still working in the medical field as a laboratory and medical technologist. When we went with the Waters, I gave up my position in the medical office where I had worked for eight years. George made arrangements for lab personnel while we were to be away. The younger daughters were still in school, and we were going "on the road" in evangelism. Boarding school was the option for the girls, so off we went with the Waters team.

Minnesota

After a day of packing and loading the big equipment truck and car we were on our way north. George and I were following the truck as we entered the southern part of Minnesota. George noticed that the truck was "dog legging" or leaning. We managed to stop Bill, and then the men surveyed the situation and began to fix things. It was a trying time with four adults, the two Waters children, and a cat and a dog to think about. To his credit Bill never uttered a harsh or discouraging word. There was calm and peace. Things eventually were repaired, and the trip went on as scheduled. I was impressed with how the problem was handled.

Unknown to George and me, Sunshine Waters was going through a medical emergency, and she had to be hospitalized for the night and day before opening night. George rose to the occasion, and with the Lord's help, he had almost everything set up and ready for Bill to begin that opening night. That was our first lesson in the challenges of evangelism and all that is involved if one is committed to doing what one is called upon to do. By the way, Mark and Wendy Waters never complained about being left at the church as George and I tried to get things done. These children simply curled up on a pew and went to sleep. They were wonderful!

My faith was beginning to build, and we plunged into the next five weeks as a team. Early on my position on the Waters team was to be pianist, vocalist, videographer, helper, and teacher for their son, Mark, and daughter, Wendy. Sunshine brought along two student desks for the children and a teacher's desk for me. I had my set of teachers' editions of every textbook that the children studied. We had fun in our classroom "on the road." We did the class work, had fun with some crafts, played games and went on field trips. We enjoyed a special trip to the capitol building in St. Paul, Minnesota, and we took in the cooking demonstrations of some of their products at the General Mills Headquarters.

The Board of Education?

We had an extra room in our apartment for the classroom, and I took great pride in making it just that: a classroom. We were very serious about the children's education. One day there was a knock at the door, and when I answered the knock, there stood a well-dressed man and woman, and with them was our building manager. The manager ostensibly told me that they were considering renting our apartment when we left in a few weeks. They came through the apartment and stopped and looked in at our classroom. I shall always suspect that they were from the board of education, and when they saw our arrangements for school, they were satisfied that the children were being taught even though they were away from home. They soon left.

George's Debut

A very interesting thing happened to George during our first campaign. Because of the fear of facing an audience, he had been firm about his not going out on stage for any reason other than the usual adjusting of mics and lights.

One night as he was standing backstage waiting for Bill to go on, on an impulse Bill pushed George through the curtain with the words, "Introduce me." Suddenly George was in front of all those people, and he needed to say something. But, what? I'm sure he was praying silently, "Help me, Dear Lord." Well, the Lord did help him get through that first appearance on stage, but it was with a lot of nervous adjusting of his glasses. I still kid him about his glasses that night. From that day onward, God has helped him overcome his stage fright. Now he appears to be at home on the stage, and at times I can't keep him off of it. Isn't that astounding for a shy guy?!

> *From that day onward, God has helped him overcome his stage fright*

George developed a strong and persuasive speaking style, and he has been instrumental in winning many people for the Lord. One of his special gifts is his ability to get decisions for the Lord in his visitations. Another hidden talent that he has found is his ability to lead singing. He found his "voice" from the Lord, and he has been nonstop with his contagious enthusiasm and energy in his zeal for evangelism. I tell him that he is my favorite song leader and evangelist to which he just grins in unbelief.

Finding His Path

Many evangelists begin their ministry in service and training with a current speaker. At this point I want to interject the fact that when George went away to college, he was somehow given incorrect counsel. He was encouraged to pursue training in the medical field. What he really had a passion for was the ministry and evangelism. That was missed somewhere in his interviews.

He had always hung around evangelists when he went to their crusades. If it meant carrying songbooks, Bibles, or carrying out the trash, he was available to help. So, he had some "catching up" to do at this time. And it was again in God's timing.

But what a whirlwind tour with Bill and Sunshine Waters! We learned so much from them, and we are indebted to them for their patience with us in the process. Sad to say, I gained about twenty pounds for which I am still paying to this day—constantly dieting. As with most evangelists and their team they miss their evening meal because of the meetings at night. Then afterwards everyone is so hungry, and that packs on pounds in a hurry. We learned to make changes in that area even if it meant giving up a nightly piece of pie at the "Poppin' Fresh" pie place there in Minneapolis. Our first crusade was now behind us. Many souls were baptized at the end of this crusade, and it was off to Florida for the next one after a brief period at home for rest and relaxation.

Florida

What a contrast! Minnesota and Florida. When we left Minnesota, it was Thanksgiving, it was eighteen degrees outside, and it was spitting snow. Florida was in the nineties and humid. Miracles happened in Minneapolis, and miracles would happen in Florida. It is always a miracle when people accept Jesus Christ as their personal Savior.

New Sabbath Keepers

We had been into the meetings in Miami, Florida, for about two weeks when two couples (two brothers and their wives) came to the meetings. "The Mark of the Beast" was being presented that first night of their attendance. These couples met with Bill after the service and announced that they had read about the meetings in the newspaper. The only thing was that the meetings hadn't been advertised in that paper, but he didn't want to argue with them. We asked them to bring us the newspaper, and they did. It was there as they said.

Another interesting thing that they revealed was that they were Sabbath keepers. So? The story goes that one of the brothers had their home for sale. It was a Sabbath afternoon, and they were inside their home with a sign on the door for any would-be buyers that read: "We are keeping the Sabbath. If you are interested in looking at our home for sale, please come back at 6:30 after sundown to see our house." He further stated that not only did the potential buyer buy their house, but also offered to pay these brothers, who are carpenters, to remodel the house for them. We learned recently that these two families are still members of that church, and the husbands serve as elders there.

What Did You Say?

Sometimes there are negative situations that happen in evangelism. Sometimes our dear, little members say the wrong things to new people.

Evangelists and their teams look at new people as babes in the Lord. These "babes" are hovered over and loved by most everyone, but occasionally, something will be spoken over them that is devastating to them.

For instance, one lady in a certain town had given her heart to Jesus and was baptized into membership of that church. She had made a decision to leave off her jewelry, but on this particular occasion she had put her earrings back on and came to church. At first many ladies are off and on again with wearing jewelry, but over time a decision is usually made to leave it off. One of the older ladies could not handle this, so she went over to the offending one, took hold of one of her ears and said, "You know you shouldn't be wearing earrings in this church!" To that remark, the earring lady left the church never to return. The ministers went to her and apologized profusely, however, the damage was done. One thing all must learn is that new people are just what they are. New. It is a growing experience, and they must be given space in which to grow and develop into mature Christians. And really, it will be a lifetime of learning and growing up into the Lord's ideal for each of us. What a privilege it is to be a part of this great family on this earth and in the earth to come when He appears.

> *One thing all must learn is that new people are just what they are. New. It is a growing experience, and they must be given space in which to grow and develop into mature Christians*

Most of the time in meetings I stayed at the piano until everyone had gone from the hall. My reasoning was that I didn't want to unknowingly say or do something that would hinder a precious soul in its decision-making time for the Lord. After that decision, then I welcomed their friendship, but until then I left the decision time to the evangelists and their assistants. After the meetings each night there was a time for input of names and sorting of tickets. We were busy with our individual duties, but on one day of the week we indulged in sightseeing and eating out.

Fun for All

One couple in a Florida congregation owned a yacht that the husband had lovingly built, and they invited our team for an overnight trip out in the bay. I'm not a sea person, however, we did enjoy the food, fun, and fellowship that was offered to us. Everywhere we went there were people who were so generous with their time and hospitality. That in itself is a real ministry—the gift of hospitality. It is certainly just as much of a blessing to modern workers for the Lord as it was to Elijah in his day and time.

Meaning Well

People will be people no matter where one goes in this world. I made many observations in our travels. I listened and learned a lot about people and perhaps they about me. Once in a campaign in the South I was standing in the foyer of a church and I overhead one of the ladies of the church say the following to a gentleman who had been attending that church for years: "Are you going to come in this time?" (Meaning, "Are you going to join the church this time?") There I stood in a state of shock at her words, but I was helpless to respond since I was only a visitor in their church as an assistant to the evangelist. I felt that she unknowingly put him in a rather embarrassing position in front of the others standing around him. I did tell the evangelist, but I don't know about the outcome of the situation. Perhaps he said something to her, but perhaps not because of possibly also embarrassing her.

Tornado Country

One of our campaigns with the Waters team led us to the Midwest. It was in May, and tornadoes were a threat. Once when Bill was visiting a prospective baptismal candidate, he came "under the siren." Fortunately for him, the tornado didn't touch down. Another time, Sunshine and I were taking a lady home from the meetings one night, and we didn't realize there was a tornado warning in effect. Blissfully, we rode on through the thunderstorm without knowing what could happen. Again, we were blessed with no tornado on the ground. George and Bill let nothing stop them in their search for the lost ones.

Seeking the Lost

One night, George and one of the church brothers were out visiting and George just happened to drive down a certain street. Suddenly Bill, his passenger, told him, "By the way, on this street there is a lady who used to be a member of our church, but it really won't do any good to visit her." Of course George insisted that they visit her, and she revealed that she had been hurt in the past by one of the members. She also stated that she had been diagnosed with breast cancer. George urged her to come to church the following night, first to talk with me for encouragement because of my medical background and issues. Then he asked her what she thought about being anointed for healing, and she was positive for that to be done.

The next night she came as promised, and she was anointed, yet, she went on to the doctor and to the hospital that week as scheduled for surgery. Later in the afternoon of the day of surgery the ministers went to check on her. The good news was that there was no sign of the cancer; however, the doctor went ahead with breast reduction due to the size of her breasts and the discomfort they were causing in her back. This lady made a renewed commitment to the Lord, and she was re-baptized. After finishing college at Collegedale, Tennessee, this lady is now a registered nurse and works in the Adventist healthcare system. Praise the Lord for her experience with Him! Miracles still happen!

A Turn in the Road

George and I were privileged to assist Bill and Sunshine Waters in several evangelistic campaigns off and on over a period of time. Perhaps there were ten in all, and each one was a thrill in seeing people surrender their hearts and lives to the Lord. Many were the wayward ones who with joy came back to God. I rejoiced with people who came up out of the water with tears of joy running down their faces. Always there were some who responded with hugs for the evangelist who had "stayed with them" through some tough times of quitting the tobacco habit. Others who had lost their way because of hurts and discouragements came back rejoicing that they were home again. It made it all worthwhile for us as the team to see these happy faces.

Many times it seems that the tobacco habit goes so very deep into a person's daily life with its tenacious clutch on the host. Some say that it is easier to stop the alcohol consumption than the smoking. This is where the Lord comes in if one is sincerely wanting to overcome the habit with His divine help. I remember how George once would set our alarm for 5:00 a. m. He would get up, call the baptismal candidate, and have a morning prayer with him before he reached for a cigarette. This man was able to stop his tobacco habit and become a member of the church.

As it inevitably happens, there comes a time when our paths take a new turn, and that is what happened in their case, and ours. Until their children could finish grade school and academy, Bill and Sunshine Waters chose to take a pastorate in Florida.

Chapter Four

Ashe County

It was the summer of 1984, and the girls had graduated academy. At that point we had come off the road for a rest and to plan what we wanted to do with our lives. The Waters children were in church school, and Bill and Sunshine were busy in their new place of service. Our then Carolina Conference President, Elder Robert Folkenberg, asked us if we wanted to go to a dark county and open up a new work.

With his encouragement we decided to move to the higher mountains of Ashe County, North Carolina. Probably no place on earth is more beautiful than the Blue Ridge Mountains in that state. Mercifully we didn't know what awaited us there. We miraculously bought twelve acres of land from a gentleman who, the next week, wondered why he had consented to sell this land to us. We felt that it was of the Lord, and we proceeded to build a house while we lived in a small mobile home during the construction of "the brown house."

> *Probably no place on earth is more beautiful than the Blue Ridge Mountains in that state. Mercifully we didn't know what awaited us there*

Living Room Evangelism

When we got the house "dried in" (able to withstand the weather), we sort of moved in while we were building. The weather turned cold, and the trailer was not adequate to keep us warm during the snowy, winter months. (Occasionally a big snow up there would measure three feet deep. The weather people didn't have us on their records as to depths of snow.) By this time, we had made many wonderful, new friends among our neighbors over and around the mountains. There was a beautiful little

Baptist church below our house, and when they had a revival George and I would attend some of their services. We loved these people and wanted to be a part of them as much as we could. They knew that we were Seventh-day Adventists, and it didn't seem to make any difference to them. In fact, it was indicated by one family that they liked for their teenage daughter to come to our house because of our being different in a good way.

At this point George put in some sawhorses in the unfinished, sub-flooring living room and laid some sheets of plywood over these to act as tables. We had Bible lessons and Bibles which would enable us to give Bible studies in this room, and we were going to invite our sweet Baptist neighbors in for these lessons. These wonderful new friends came to our studies, and ten of them completed the course and received certificates of completion.

Can you imagine how frustrating it was for George and me because these dear ones saw God's truths, but they didn't "see" them? Because of the religious traditions of the mountains, it was difficult for them to see that the Sabbath made a difference for them. I remember one sweet lady who would start a mild sentence of disagreement with: "But I believe…" She would say all of this so softly as if she didn't want to hurt our feelings. We had been told that colporteurs had been all through that part of the world, and that Adventist books were everywhere up there. In the county itself, some "inroads" were made, and baptisms resulted. We just had to remain friends with these sweet people and leave the harvest to someone else. That is the marvelous thing about our God! He gave us the freedom of choice, and we could only urge them just so far in making decisions to follow the Lord into new truths. We knew that these people were Christians, and we also knew that they were steeped in long-standing family relationships and traditions.

Bluegrass Musicians for the Lord

We were getting to know many people around the county through music ministry. The gospel is recorded in many songs and hymns, and we felt that we could reach some of the people through the medium of song. Our friends, Russ and Nan Sturgill, went with us to Ashe County. This couple had retired as traveling musicians to the schools in that part of the world. They played several "Bluegrass" type instruments, and for what the four of us wanted to do, I learned to play some of the instruments as well. They played banjo, dulcimer, autoharp, guitar and mandolin. I learned mandolin, guitar, and autoharp, and I also had a portable keyboard, marimba, and vibraharp. George was in charge of our sound. So, we formed a vocal and instrumental group and began to go to the churches as we were invited for some musical outreach.

The Running Preacher Man

One night the four of us visited a Baptist church in the Wolf Knob community where a revival was in progress. We took along our instruments and gave a thirty-minute concert. Then the "preacher" started preaching. At about halfway through his sermon he was preaching his heart out to the people and was overcome with emotion. Some strong emotion! At that point he ran outdoors and turned around and ran back in again (still preaching as he ran). The significant thing to know was that he had worked all day cutting down trees, and as he ran by us, we almost lost our breath from his body odor. Apparently, he forgot to shower and change clothes before he came to preach that night. One sweet church member told us after the service that we sounded like angels singing. Such an interesting evening.

A Hell-Fire Sermon

The four of us had wanted to visit a Mennonite church down along the highway going into West Jefferson, North Carolina. When we arrived at the church, we discovered that a local Baptist minister had been invited to speak there that night. He recognized us as Adventists; thus, he changed his sermon topic to "Payday Someday," or better known as a sermon on "hell." During his sermon he exclaimed: "I don't care what Adventists say! 'Payday Someday.'" He made a mistake in saying that because the pastor of this church was now our friend. After the service this pastor cornered the visiting minister with these words, "You shouldn't have preached as you did tonight. These Adventists are our friends. You probably have offended them." When he told us about all of this, we assured him that we were not offended. We just smiled and departed for home.

A few years later a young Mennonite pastor was working on a car at his garage, and it suddenly fell against him and broke both his legs. He was a good mechanic, and several times he had come to our house to repair a minor problem with our car. During one of these times, I offered him some of our Adventist literature. I was sad when he refused the gift. Jesus is sad when we refuse His gift to us.

An Asbestos Body?

At another Baptist church a statement was made by the visiting minister that none of us had ever heard used in defense of an ever-burning hell. The

Baptist evangelist said, "I believe that God gives sinners something like an asbestos body so that they burn forever and ever." This man knew that we were Adventists and changed his sermon to the topic of hell. I've always wished that in circumstances such as this that one of us could somehow take the floor and explain to the people how it really will be, that sinners won't burn forever. They didn't read their Bibles, and we knew that for a fact. They seemed to be content to let these preachers tell them error and believe it. At least this Baptist evangelist knew some logic in what he was saying. He had to make it fit their doctrine of burning forever and ever.

The funerals that we attended contained the same errors. We went to several during the time that we lived there, and usually at the beginning of the eulogy they preached the deceased on into heaven. However, by the time the service was ending they had them going to the grave where they would rise and meet their loved ones on the resurrection morning. Again, we longed to tell these dear people the truth, and many times we were given the opportunity on personal contacts.

The Light Shines Brightly in a "Dark County"

Ashe County was a "dark county" spiritually most of all, and it was also deprived socially, economically, and educationally speaking. This assignment suited George and me just fine because we liked the challenges of new adventures. We and three other couples began to lay plans for a congregation in this beautiful place.

I remember well the night when the eight of us met in one of our homes for an organizational meeting. We laughed as we first nominated one and then the other for a position in our "new" church. It all ended by each having to take multiple jobs. We intended from the start that we would be known as a church group. We didn't like the term "company" because we felt that term limited us too much in the goals and plans that we had.

Ashe County was a "dark county" spiritually most of all, and it was also deprived socially, economically, and educationally speaking. This assignment suited George and me just fine because we liked the challenges of new adventures

The conference president and the conference committee must have been very amused when we showed up for our meeting with them. We came armed with a map that showed a red light where all of us lived and where any prospects lived. We were granted church status, and off we went to conquer Ashe County. We were anxious to get a church built so that we could begin evangelistic meetings and do outreach of some kind.

At first we met in the community center in Warrensville, North Carolina. Then we started growing as a group, and the Methodist congregation there in Warrensville graciously rented their charming, historic church to us until our church was finished. Toward the end of our construction they dropped the rent fee as their gift to our church building program. Subsequently, our members did raise the funds, and a lovely sanctuary was built which sits beside a meandering creek. We even had a footbridge over this stream to our church which many people have attended over the years. This church was built with great pride of accomplishment. One of our elders, Dr. Ron Haupt, had seen a similar church via television from Switzerland during the Olympics that year. From that inspiration he drew the plans for our church, and it was a great team effort to see the completion of this project. I think it is the most beautiful Adventist church in the Carolinas.

Wading out into Deep Waters

George had done a little speaking on the Waters team, but not much. It was in this Warrensville church in this dark county that he really "got his feet wet" in preaching, so to speak. God was preparing him little by little for what he would be doing as time went by. At the encouragement of the pastor who couldn't be at our church but every other week, the men of the church began filling in with messages to us from the Lord, and George was one of them. Pastor Larry Allen said he couldn't do all that needed to be done, and that he was counting on these laymen to help with the speaking. They rose to the task, and we were blessed.

Life and Near-Death Experiences

During construction of this church George and I experienced some life-threatening circumstances. One weekend in 1986, George suffered severe stomach pains. At first we thought that it was a flu-like illness. On Sunday morning he was in such great pain that he finally relented and asked me to drive him to the hospital that was an hour away in Boone, North Carolina. On the way he exclaimed every time that I hit a bump. (At that time part of the road into our home was a dirt road.) He also begged me to hurry. I drove madly down the highway and into the entrance to the emergency room. I got him into a wheelchair and pushed him toward a nurse with the words: "He is sick." George had already turned gray by this time. After a quick examination the doctor came out and informed me that George's colon had ruptured and that surgery was imminent. I cried and cried. Then I prayed.

Several hours later the surgeon reappeared with the news that a large portion of George's colon was removed and that a colostomy bag had been put in place while he recuperated. I will say that the Lord was so good to have spared George's life during that awful emergency. (It was thought that the colon ruptured after George had taken an aspirin-like pill.)

About midnight that night after his surgery he was awakened by voices in the hall beside his room. That patient was Doctor Haupt, who was wanting to see George. He was saying, "I want to see George! I want to see George!" The doctor had enjoyed riding his motorcycle that day, but he had an accident which left him with a broken hand and other injuries. There was nothing doing until the nurse rolled him into George's room where these two church brothers in the Lord discussed the events of that day. Doctor Haupt did, thankfully, recover well in the following weeks.

After a few days in the hospital, George was discharged to go home; though, before I could drive him home I took him, in his pajamas, to K-Mart to buy some pants to fit him after this surgery. Later, when he went back for the colostomy repair, that surgery took eight hours. As you can imagine, the surgeon was completely worn out from the ordeal. George had earlier told the surgeon that he healed rather fast, but the surgeon chose to ignore that comment for professional reasons and delayed the procedure too long. Adhesions were everywhere in George's abdomen, and they had to be removed. In my limited medical knowledge, I could only guess at the extent of the "repair job." From that day onward, George has never had any more trouble with his colon.

Tried as by Fire

But my turn came in 1987. My husband had mostly recuperated, and we were working as diligently on the church as we could. I remember feeling so very tired. I hate to confess this, but just to keep going, I was sometimes drinking four or five soft drinks on the days that I went to work on the church. (No one knew that I was drinking that many sodas.) My job was painting the windows and trim, and they told me that I was the best one for that job. Since then I have wondered if they were just telling me that to keep me working! No, they were such good friends, and I believe that they meant that. I was a very slow, deliberate painter, and it did give me a good feeling of accomplishment as I finished each window and board. I painted to follow the grain of the wood.

The dedication of the new church took place in September of 1987. It was a beautiful ceremony with the conference officers in attendance. They asked me to write the dedication song and sing it for the occasion. I thought everything was going well; still, I felt like I was going to collapse during the whole service.

Earlier in the summer I had experienced a large swelling under my left arm. Three doctors diagnosed me with an infection or a sebaceous cyst. Isn't that astounding! I even took a round of penicillin. But the "swelling" persisted, so on my own I went to George's surgeon for a check-up. Nancy Reagan had come forward with her news about her breast cancer, and this somehow gave me courage to just go and see about my situation. The news wasn't good. (I hope I am encouraging some reader of this account to take charge of any questionable places on your body. Don't hesitate. Just go and see about it. Put your case into the hands of God.)

After the examination, surgery was scheduled and performed. A pathologist studied the specimen from this excision, and the surgeon called us by phone with the news that it was a carcinoma, a huge carcinoma. (Since George is a lab technologist, he wanted to see the specimen. He later told me that it looked like a large mushroom.) Back to the story: The surgeon also stated that it might have metastasized to other parts of my body, and that I might not have more than nine months in which to live. I was terrified. I wanted to serve the Lord in this new place, and I thought, "What is happening to me?"

An Angel?

That night I went out on our deck to talk with the Lord. (As I write this, I still feel some of the emotions that I felt that night out under the stars that were created so long ago by our Creator.) I was experiencing a fine tremor just under my skin over my entire body. I was very serious with the Lord. I talked and talked with Him out there. George was in the house doing his talking with Him. After some time, we lay down in bed for the night. Still, I was trembling inside, and by that time I was visibly shaking all over. I decided to sleep in the guest room so that George could get his rest that night.

As I lay there in the guest room, I asked my guardian angel to hold my hand. (I know that we don't pray to angels, but for that night, I felt better just knowing that my angel was there beside me. The scripture verse that says "Perfect love casteth out all fear" came into my mind, but I couldn't remember where it was found in the Bible. I asked for it to be shown to me. Then I picked up my Bible from the table, opened it, and there in front of me was the text: 1 John 4:18. "There is no fear in love; but perfect love casteth out fear: because fear hath torment. He that feareth is not made perfect in love."

Perhaps that text can be applied in another way for some other person, but for me, it was a powerful consolation that night back in October of 1987. I knew that I loved God, and I was counting on His perfect love for me to cast out my fear. I truly believe that my angel guided my fingers in opening up the Bible right to that text. I will always believe that. When I get to heaven I want to ask my angel about it. The miracle of that night was that the trembling stopped, and I slept like a baby.

The Bright Light

The next day George was to go back into town some sixty miles away to get some pre-test supplies for me for my scheduled CT scan on Thursday. They were endeavoring to find the primary site for this huge mass that was excised from under my left arm. Later he was to tell me that on the way to town and on the way back that he had invited our Lord Jesus to sit in the passenger seat as they traveled. George said that he talked with his unseen passenger about our lives and how he wasn't wanting to lose me. I believe that George made some commitments to the Lord that he would serve Him more faithfully if only He, the Lord, would take charge of my situation.

As I said before, the doctor had said that I probably had only nine months in which to live. George was terrified. I was terrified, but I tried to stay calm for his sake. George and I loved each other very much—more than we had realized, I think. His brush with death a year earlier had only cemented our bond of love. We discovered that storms and trials endured together do draw us, first of all, closer to God. Secondly, it strengthens the earthly ties with our spouse and with our families.

So on Wednesday I drank the medicine that had been prescribed for my cleansing due to the CT scan the next day. George had asked for my healing, and his footnote to his earlier prayer was: "Lord, if she is cancer free, please let a bright light be around her as she leaves the scanning room." George was so confident of the results that he told the surgeon that they wouldn't find any cancer. The surgeon said, "We'll have to wait and see."

George said that as I walked out of the scanning room, there was a light around me so bright that he couldn't clearly see me. I was oblivious to all of this at that time. The report later came back, and no primary site was ever found. It was negative. The cancer team insisted that I follow up surgery with radiation and chemotherapy. Two Adventist doctors who were friends of ours concurred with this advice, so I chose to undergo treatments. In hindsight, I shall always wonder about my decision to do all of that—would I have gotten well without the damaging chemo and radiation therapy?

In one of my follow-up examinations, a silver-colored area showed up on my mammogram, and my surgeon thought that it looked suspicious. He ordered a needle biopsy. I'm a rather stoic person, and when the radiologist was inserting a needle down into my left breast to the suspicious area, he stopped and with a wild-eyed look said, "Doesn't this hurt?" (It did hurt because I chose to undergo this procedure without an anesthetic.) I said very calmly, "Proceed." He couldn't believe that I was saying nothing with regard to pain. The amazing thing to tell you is: The needle biopsy results were negative. Prior to this procedure, George and I had gone to Florida where Bill Waters anointed me and prayed for me that this would be negative. I truly believe the Lord had healed me!

Let no one tell you that there is such a thing as a "nothing to it" attitude with regard to chemotherapy and radiation. These procedures do their work, but the side effects can be overwhelming. Most women feel very strongly about their hair. I do. It sort of defines who we are physically, speaking as to our personality and our total look of womanhood. And when one of us has a "bad hair day," our family and friends know it by how it affects us and our moods.

Each time that I went to the medical office for any procedure, I couldn't help noticing the other patients who were wearing different hats and scarves. One would have to live through "that experience" to really know how each of us felt during that time of helplessness and resignation. Perhaps you wonder why I am telling you this part of my journey. It is part of the warp and woof that make up the person I seem to be with my struggles and victories. These determine how one reacts to future events, and maybe, just maybe, it might help someone hold on when holding on seems "pretty near impossible."

But back to the story: The chemotherapy caused my hair to come out or fall out. When it started coming out, I helped it along by pulling it out by handfuls. This upset George, and he couldn't understand why I was doing that. But I thought, "If it has to be, let's just get it over with." When he came up to our bedroom and caught me pulling out strands of hair, I laughed and said, "Instead of singing 'O That Silver-Haired Mother of Mine' our girls can sing 'O That Bald-Headed Mother of Mine.'" With that said, I fell across our bed literally wailing to the top of my voice. George did his best to console me through that storm. I am not relating this to get pity from my readers. It is to let you feel and experience what cancer victims go through. That storm passed over with its thunder and lightning, and life continued on with the Lord Jesus ever with me.

But on the brighter side, I will reveal to you a very sweet, private moment with my husband. One Sabbath afternoon we stretched out for a nap after coming home from church and eating lunch. When I awoke George was sitting up in bed with a book; however, he was just sitting there staring down at me. I looked up at him, and I sleepily said, "Why are you looking at me?" To which he replied, "I was just looking at how beautiful you are!" What a darling, sweet man! I had been asleep, and I was bald, yet, he loved me enough to reassure me of a continuing love and acceptance amid such awful circumstances. The Lord saw us through. Praise His wonderful name! As I write this, it has been thirty-two years since that time and place. Currently, I have had to have much remedial surgery for the side effects from the radiation. So be it.

> *That storm passed over with its thunder and lightning, and life continued on with the Lord Jesus ever with me*

(It's amazing what one will find when going through boxes of memorabilia. In 1991, our local newspaper sponsored a "Sweetheart" contest, and the rules stated that the letter had to be very concise. My letter was chosen as the winner of this competition and prizes were awarded from local merchants. The prizes were very nice, and I was grateful for them; however, the prize was already won before I entered the "race," and that was my husband, George. The letter:

TO MY DARLING HUSBAND, GEORGE:

Dear George, Why do I call you my sweetheart? That's an easy question to answer: You were there when the surgery was performed. In the days that followed when chemotherapy made me ill, you held my hand. When my hair came out, you said I was still beautiful. You were the silver lining in my clouds. What a man you are that you could show such love and tenderness! You're my sweetheart, and I love you! This is my tribute to you, my wonderful husband. Your wife, Charlotte.)

I don't know why my appearance shone so brightly that day after my CT scan. The only other time that this happened was in later years in an evangelistic campaign in south Florida. I was giving a young woman a religious book, and suddenly she looked at me in astonishment and said, "Your face is shining." I wasn't aware of anything different about myself. I only knew what she was saying. Perhaps the Lord had something to do with that incident for this woman's benefit and just used me because I was near her. I don't know.

We Are Loved No Matter What

We can't begin to know the mind and ways of the Lord. I've often wondered just what the chastening of the Lord really is. Does He allow pain and suffering to happen to draw us nearer to Him? Someone said that it was to redirect a person in some new course of action. Some have wondered if things are sent on people as punishment. I know one thing: God loves me. God loves you and all of us. The story of His love starts in Genesis and ends in Revelation. If we only had one verse—John 3:16—we would know that He loves us:

> *"For God so loved the world, that he gave his only begotten Son, that whosoever believeth in him should not perish, but have everlasting life."*

Whatever the reason for all these physical, emotional, and mental hardships, George and I yielded under the mighty hand of God. We certainly wanted His ultimate will in our lives. It makes me think of a sentence in the book *Help In Daily Living* by Ellen G. White which says: "God never leads His children otherwise than they would choose to be led, if they could see the end from the beginning, and discern the glory of the purpose which they are fulfilling as coworkers with Him" (p. 11). I do know that we called upon Him and promised Him that we would serve

Him all the days that He had for us. We have made many mistakes. We have fallen short of what He would have wanted for us, but someday Jesus will be coming back, and we want to be found in His service wherever He would want us to be.

Another aspect of pain and suffering to consider is the fact that others are watching our reactions and how we deal with our allotted circumstances. Unknown to me, my sister was intently watching these events in our lives: first, George's surgery and recuperation, then mine. My sister is now deceased. She never accepted this Sabbath message and the other truths that we have come to love. She was a Christian, and I have given her to the Lord. But her comment one day was: "Charlotte, you and George have had first one thing and another to deal with, but you seem to just pick up and keep on going." I don't know how those who don't know the Lord "just keep on going." I believe He is our Strength, and that is what undergirded our faith in Him through it all. Praise His name!

"When It Rains, It Pours"

One nice summer day George and I were just busy around the house when the telephone rang. Bill and Sunshine called to see if we could drop everything and go with them on a crusade out in the Midwest. We packed and made provisions for our house and animals' care, and off we went for a six-weeks stay for a wonderful evangelistic effort.

But at our Warrensville, North Carolina church, plans had been made for a one-week revival by speaker Dr. Dan Jarrard. This was scheduled for when we got back home at the close of our crusade with the Waters. We were en route home when we got word that George's father was extremely ill in Tennessee, and George should come to his bedside as soon as we could get back home in North Carolina. When we got back and unpacked, George left for his parents' home to be with his dad.

Dr. Dan Jarrard arrived, and the meetings began at our church, minus George. The couple who had consented to share their home with Dan during the crusade suddenly left for California. That meant that Dan transferred over to our house.

As George left for Tennessee, he had given me instructions to drive to Bristol, Virginia, on a business errand for him. He gave me some money and said, "Drive over to Bristol for me, and then take Dan with you to the cafeteria where the two of you can have lunch." I drove to Bristol, took care of the business for George, then we went to lunch. While we were sitting there, a fine tremor came over me, and I think that I was near a physical collapse from the exhaustion of the "log jam" that had come our way. We were delighted to have Dan, but I was completely "out of steam." I looked at Dan and said, "Dan, here are the keys to the car. You will have to drive us back to the house. I am unable to drive."

Dan was a wonderful houseguest, and his wife, Rebecca, joined us a little later in the week. George's father improved, and George returned home for the last two nights of the revival. It all worked out in the end, but for a little while things were tight. Situations can happen in evangelism that you aren't counting on. We began to wonder what would be next in our ever-changing lives.

Chapter Five

Overseas and Back

1988 found us just day-to-day living in the brown house, going to church weekly, and my trying to gain back my health and strength. By this time we had started raising goats, and a little later llamas just for the fun of it. Working with these fun and interesting animals caused me to get out into the great outdoors to care for them. That fall the mountains just showed themselves with their colorful autumn dresses. Everywhere we looked there was color. (During that time George happened to be outside working when he saw a commercial airliner drop its altitude and fly at an angle so that the passengers could see all this color.) I felt so wonderful in spite of what had just happened to me in my battle with breast cancer. God is so good! As I look back to that time, I truly believe that God in His loving kindness and mercy placed George and me in that peaceful and serene setting for our time of need. We went through the fire, but it was on the side of a majestic mountain of His creation. All this constantly pointed us up to Him.

Onward and Upward

Late in 1988, Bill and Sunshine Waters gave us an S. O. S. call for help with a crusade in southeast Georgia. We loaded up our old motor home and headed out once again on the evangelism trail. It was so refreshing to be back with the people. The meetings went well, and many were converted and baptized. We had helped in the Oklahoma meeting, so we were "on call" whenever we were needed.

Whenever I overheard George's telephone conversations with Bill Waters I knew what was to be. Usually before they were finished talking I was at the piano gathering music to take with us. We have been known to leave in a day's time. In 1984, George formed his own medical equipment business to give us more flexibility. This meant that he could arrange things so that we could be away on evangelistic trips as needed, and there were many of these times.

The Awesome Invitation

This worked especially well for a very exciting invitation that we received in 1992. The Berlin Wall had come down and invitations were being extended to evangelists to go abroad to former unfriendly places. Evangelist Harmon Brownlow and his wife, Margaret, on the Waters' recommendation, invited George and me to accompany them on an evangelistic campaign in Kishinev, Moldova, a former republic of the former U.S.S.R. We accepted, made our arrangements, and traveled with them to that faraway place. My role was pianist and soloist, and George was to be Doctor Brownlow's assistant in any way that was needed.

Doctor Harmon Brownlow had been a football star at The Citadel, a university near Charleston, South Carolina, in his young adulthood. After his conversion he felt the call from God to preach the gospel. Along the way he met an influential, elderly Adventist attorney who became his mentor in things pertaining to the Sabbath and other Adventist doctrines. He was subsequently baptized, graduated Southern Missionary College, and later went to seminary fulfillment for his degree. He was ordained as a minister of the gospel in the Seventh-day Adventist Church.

By that time we had been through many crusades, and in some places we were almost tested by fire. After an arduous trip, we arrived in Kishinev, Moldova. We found that the meetings were to be held in a very spectacular auditorium. The concert grand piano sat proudly on the stage as if it was just waiting for me to glide my fingers over its keys. Talking about evangelism! I felt that I was almost "in heaven" with just the thought of once again playing for an evangelistic crusade. My childhood dream was realized over and over again. God is so good!

The Ghilenskis

The host family for George and me was the Ghilenski family, consisting of the parents, Tamara and Vasily, and two sons, ages thirteen and eleven. This very hospitable Moldovan couple gave us their lovely furnished bedroom in their apartment home for all of our stay of six weeks. The parents slept on a sofa bed in the sitting room, and the boys slept on a similar sofa in the other sitting/work room. The customs were altogether different from ours. The food was different, and the bathroom accommodations were different, much different! We were treated to borsht with lots of cabbage juice and possibly a chicken foot thrown in and the bathroom was like nothing we see here in the United States. The toilet was simply a hole in the ground! There was a lot of adapting on our part, but we managed well.

We especially became attached to the two young Ghilenski boys, Dima and Genia. We played with them and laughed with them, and they quickly responded to our overtures with love in return. One day we were about to enjoy Tamara's chicken borscht when I noticed little Dima was gnawing on a chicken foot. That tore at my heart to see that when I knew in America chicken feet weren't special. There is no nourishment in a chicken foot, is there? In an instant, I cut myself a sliver of the thigh in my bowl, and I silently laid the rest over into Dima's bowl. No one said a word. I thought to myself, "A chicken foot? My mother threw those away." Any one of you would have done just what I did. You would have thought of the child and reacted quickly.

> *One day we were about to enjoy Tamara's chicken borscht when I noticed little Dima was gnawing on a chicken foot. That tore at my heart to see that when I knew in America chicken feet weren't special*

The Brownlows stayed in the home of the wife of a deceased army captain. Harmon is quite tall, and the narrow single beds in their bedroom were almost hazardous for him at times. One night he fell off the backside of his bed onto the floor, whereupon he had much difficulty getting up again because of the suspicious maze of wires on the floor. These were things that happened that caused us to laugh a lot. This house where they stayed was in the older section of Moldova; therefore, the accommodations were not so modern as those where we stayed.

Opening Night in Kishinev, Moldova

We had come as a team to Kishinev on an invitation from the union president there. We were far, far from home, and we wanted good attendance at our meetings. It was Friday night—opening night! Opening night is always an event for ministers and their teams. Will the people come? Did we advertise properly?

Clomp! Clomp! Tramp! Tramp! Click! Click! Are those footsteps coming up the marble stairs? Yes, they are coming! The people are coming! Men in heavy boots and women in high-heeled boots! They are coming! They are arriving early by streetcar, by buses, by car. Those are wonderful sounds of footsteps finding their way up and into that beautiful auditorium. One lady was ascending the stairs with crutches. Another lady was in a wheelchair and was being carried up the stairs in her chair. We thought, "The people will be so comfortable seated in the mauve-colored chairs with their feet resting on the intricate design of the wood floor. The soft light from the intricate chandeliers will be restful to their eyes as they sit and listen to the soft, spiritual music being played on the concert grand piano by an American lady who, by this time, was in awe of this marvelous situation.

At 7:00 o'clock the coordinator began by welcoming the people—over one thousand of them. As he was explaining the attendance card, he said, "It is all right to put your name on it. You will not be turned in to the KGB." I thought, "Is that a joke or are they still around?"

There is a music conservatory in Kishinev, and some of the students contributed much to the meetings in the way of choral music and string ensembles. The quality of music in Moldova is superb, and the ardor with which the people sing stirs deep feelings within one's heart. The music reflected the sorrow and hardships which the people have endured over the years, and their music is one way in which they can express themselves. Most of their music is written in a minor key which is somewhat sad to me. Most of the music that I presented was written in a major key. I had many, many requests for copies of the music that I took over there. If I should ever go back to that part of the world again, I would take more written music. Much of what I played was "by ear" with no written music at all.

One highlight was meeting a musician by the name of Sergei who was a graduate of the Moscow Conservatory of Music. He was the featured pianist at an international hotel in Kishinev each night. The auditorium was multi-purpose, and Sergei arrived to play piano for a wedding that was scheduled in another section there. The only thing was the lack of a piano, and he thought to move the auditorium one out into the wedding site. When I told him that wouldn't be possible, he just gave up that idea and began to get interested in what we were doing.

I taught him the words and music to *"Amazing Grace,"* which caused him to inquire as to what does this "Amazing Grace" mean? Dr. Brownlow briefly explained the plan of salvation to him before the meeting began that night. Thereafter he attended several meetings. (This young man had never before heard a hymn or the gospel as it is found in Jesus Christ.) I was delighted to have him accompany me as I presented that song one night. After I got back home to America, I sent my complete score of Handel's *"The Messiah"* back to him via another team which was traveling there for another crusade. I could only give him to the Lord after we left.

Opening night was a wonderful experience from beginning to the end. There was much excitement and anticipation on the part of the audience. Dr. Brownlow accepted the challenge of working with two translators very well, considering the fact that two dominant languages were spoken in Moldova: Russian and Romanian. His messages were beautiful messages that spoke of the love of God. Doctrinal lectures were included in the series. These dear people needed lots of encouragement and hope.

Bibles and Baptisms

A week into the meetings on Friday night the people who attended were scheduled to begin studying the Bible with the aid of lessons. It was an experience that I shall never forget! In that first week, Dr. Brownlow had proclaimed the love of God for this planet in sending His Son, Jesus, to die for all mankind. He established the veracity of the Bible by references to nature and fulfilled prophecy, and he truly preached his heart out each night to a waiting congregation. They kept coming night after night; some were even there two hours before the service. Such a soul-hunger for the Word of God!

Most of the people sat in the same chair each night; therefore, I began to recognize a few from my seat at the piano. There they sat night after night with their expectant faces turned to the stage as sheep waiting to be fed. No matter the weather—they came. Sometimes it was cold in the auditorium—they stayed. They were dressed in boots, warm stockings, heavy coats, woolen scarves, and fur hats. It was almost as if they were saying, "We're fine. Just tell us, again and again, Dr. Brownlow. We have suffered from spiritual starvation so long. Feed us with the Living Word, please, again and again!"

These dear people were handed the Word of God, the Bible, and the Bible lessons around 6:40 that Friday night, and that part of the program was to have been over at 7:00. At 7:00, Dr. Brownlow and the two translators came out to begin the main service. There was too much excitement among the people. They were chattering among themselves and showing each other passages from the Bible. Just having the lessons would have caused quite a stir, but a Bible?!! One could feel the joy among the people.

How would anyone in America have felt to be handed his or her Bible for the very first time in his or her own language? It would be hard to contain the excitement over such an event. The Russian translator, Victoria, motioned for me to play the piano some more while the people endeavored to settle down. It took a full ten minutes or more of playing before the service could go on. It was a very moving experience! I'm very happy to have had the privilege of witnessing that one event, and it made me want to read and study more.

The first baptism had the same effect on the team as did the first Bible class. It was held on Sabbath morning, November 28, 1992, immediately after Sabbath School. Never will I forget it! The baptismal pool was a round army-surplus holding tank made of camouflage fabric. The pastors had built steps going down into the pool and out on the other side. The choir was in place and singing a song in a minor key. Presently the candidates marched out onto the stage in double file and dressed in their white robes. It was a very emotional moment—somehow I fought back the tears.

On the other side of the stage there had been tears. Dr. Brownlow had earlier invited the baptismal candidates to come backstage and prepare for their baptism. There were thirty-one people who had given their hearts to the Lord and had studied the Bible more in depth in readiness for baptism. These were the first fruits; however, approximately one hundred extra people came backstage to also experience baptism. With tears rolling down his cheeks, the evangelist had to explain to these dear people that only the thirty-one would be baptized that day. He explained that there would be another baptism the following week, and that they would be studied with in preparation.

Many of the people had been under the impression that just merely being baptized meant their ticket to heaven. They needed more instruction from the pastors in the Bible classes and from the pulpit by the speaker. He felt compassion for them in their sincere desire for baptism.

After this first baptism, one lady came up to me while I was playing piano and began hugging and kissing me while speaking to me in her language that I didn't understand. Although I did understand that she was crying and rejoicing, and I just stopped playing, and I began to cry and rejoice with her. About that time we were summoned as a team out on the stage. I walked out with tears flowing down my face. What a day!

The Villages

We were in Moldova for over six weeks, and the Lord mightily blessed our efforts there. And what an experience! Several times we were taken to other villages to see the churches and meet some of the members. The pastors from these village churches were the helpers for the meetings held in Kishinev. George became very good friends with Victor, the pastor of the Gura Galbenei Church, and Victor invited George to come out on our day off and speak at his church.

First we were taken to another pastor's home where supper was served to us and to others in our party. As we pulled into the driveway where supper was to be served, we were greeted by a group of ladies who were all smiles. The hostess came toward us with the traditional big bread and salt reception. This tradition began years ago when farm wives would leave bread and salt for any possible visitor who might be hungry while the family was working in the fields. One is expected to pinch off a morsel of bread, dip it in the cup of salt, and eat it.

We were invited inside where we promptly removed our shoes. The Moldovans usually place beautiful Oriental rugs on their floors which they fiercely protect. That day was George's birthday, and so these pastors and wives were honoring him. We were seated at a long table laden with turkey, potato salad, pea salad, eggplant, cheeses, olives, fruit, chai, etc.

At the end of the meal we stood while the host and his wife presented George with flowers and a Moldovan pottery teapot. This teapot was in the shape of a chicken with six small teacups hanging from hooks on each side of this chicken. The significance of this pottery was the fact that it had been in their family for years, and they were giving it to George as a gift. (Later, en route home to America, I carried this chicken through every airport in George's camera case. It now sits in our kitchen high on a shelf.)

After this wonderful meal, it was time for us to leave for Victor's church where George was to speak. The purpose of the meeting was for him to speak and then invite people to come to Jesus and later begin Bible studies. There was a huge crowd at the church when we arrived. My physical need at that moment was a restroom. Theodor, our translator, found a lady to escort me outside and to the block building at the far side of the church property. The cold north wind was blowing across that hilltop in icy blasts. Before we left America someone had related an experience to me about the holes in the floor in some of the outside restrooms. When we went in, sure enough, there was a hole in the floor in each doorless compartment. It met my needs, and we darted back through the cold night to the church.

I had on my coat, gloves, and my fur-lined boots, but I had brought heels to change into for the services. I removed my boots, but I put them right back on—there was no heat in the building. The people sat in church bundled up in full-dress winter clothes and never complained. The singing was vigorous and happy, and no one seemed in any hurry. George spoke with just his dress coat on, but I'm sure he was cold. There were many who decided to engage further in Bible studies which began the next week.

These meetings in Moldova will have a harvest that none of us will ever fully know on this earth. After the meeting we were taken to the fellowship room for hot borscht and a fruit drink. Nothing was wasted. The leftovers from our plates were put back into the pot to be reheated and served later. What a birthday to remember with new friends on the other side of the earth. Someday we hope to see them again in heaven.

A Moldovan Historic Event

One afternoon something happened that caused quite a bit of excitement in the Ghilenski household. Tamara received a phone call, and after she hung up, she found her dictionary and frantically searched for a word or phrase to explain to me what was going on. Finally she found the word "here" and said, "Kulakov, here." I still didn't know what was she was saying, but later in the day we discovered that not only was Elder Kulakov coming to their apartment to dine, but also Elder and Mrs. Robert Folkenberg, Elder and Mrs. Ted Wilson, and another couple would be coming.

Elder Kulakov was resigning as President of the Euro-Asia Division, and Elder Ted Wilson was being introduced to the union divisions as the new president, and he was accompanied by his wife, Nancy. Traveling with them was a couple from Arkansas. All of these people were to be guests at "our place" the next day.

When I saw Tamara and Vasile's banquet table the next day I cried at the beauty of it and the excitement of having our leaders and their wives with us. Dr. and Mrs. Brownlow and Elder Marvin Lowman were also invited to join our group for the occasion. We had read about Elder Kulakov in some of our church papers, and George and I were thrilled at finally meeting this mighty man of God. It was wonderful having, at that time, our General Conference President, Elder Robert Folkenberg, and his wife, Anita, with us. Elder and Mrs. Wilson were very cordial, and looking back, it truly was a historic time in our Adventist history. To think that in the future from that time that Elder Wilson would assume the awesome position of World President of our church. Accompanying them was the very warm and friendly couple from Arkansas, U. S. A. We felt it a real privilege to have all of these guests with us during our campaign in Moldova.

On Sabbath at the auditorium Elder Folkenberg was to introduce Elder Wilson to the Moldovan members gathered there for Sabbath services. The Folkenbergs, the Wilsons, and many pastors were opposite me on the other side of the stage. A choir was in place on the stage that presented several beautiful arrangements to add to the beauty of the service. George came around to where I was seated at the piano and told me what Elder Folkenberg was going to sing before he spoke. George continued his instructions by saying that I was to be ready with the music introduction "at a moment's notice." I remember that he blessed the people with "He Touched Me" by Bill and Gloria Gaither. (The language barrier was such that we had to rely on a translator or interpreter for our instructions as to what was next on the program.)

The wonderful Moldovans rejoiced that they had the privilege of having these distinguished guests in their remote part of the world, and the team rejoiced with them. How could we ever forget the excitement of that weekend!

Farewell!

The camaraderie that developed between the Moldovan pastors and the American pastors was clearly seen early in the daily workers' meetings. On our team was a minister from the Midwest, Pastor Marvin Lowman, who had come along on this crusade to assist. Dr. Brownlow had the first devotional, and thereafter it was rotated between him, Pastor Lowman, and George.

It fell George's lot to give the final devotional on the last Friday morning to these new pastor friends. These men had labored together for those last few weeks; they had laughed together; they had cried together; they had rejoiced together over what the Lord had done. Now it was all coming to an end, and each one there that day was in a reflective mood. With Theodor at his side to translate, George began his charge:

> *This is our last time together in just this way. Never will we meet again just like this*

"This is our last time together in just this way. Never will we meet again just like this. The fellowship that we have had must be something like the early church members had together. They had one purpose: the spread of the gospel." George continued, "I have thought a lot about what Dr. Brownlow said about the 'foolishness of preaching.' Colossians 1:21. It is true! There is no speaker in America, or in the world, who could keep a crowd coming night after night after night to hear that speaker talk on any subject other than the gospel of Jesus Christ our Lord. There is power in the name of Jesus. His story never gets old. Children hear it at their mother's knee; they hear it over and over again as they grow through childhood and into adulthood. If they yield their lives to God, the story will grow sweeter and sweeter right into old age.

"The promise and hope of our Redeemer coming back looms bright on the horizon. May all these thoughts help keep your sermons fresh and new to your congregations. May this campaign fuel a fire in your bones that will spill over into the lives of your members that they, too, will spread the good news of the gospel all over Moldova and into all the world.'"

Then George softened his voice for the remaining final words. "We truly hate to leave this place. We can honestly say, 'It was good for us to have been here!' Although we feel regrets at leaving you, we, at the same time can hardly wait to get back to America to give them the good report of the work of God here in Moldova. You may be sure that you will always be a part of us. You are etched in our memory now, and we would find it hard to forget you. May God send you a double portion of His Holy Spirit as you continue the good work that He has begun in you. Guard the flock well! May we be together around the throne soon.'"

Simultaneously the men stood and applauded as George finished his charge to them. There were many eyes brimming with tears. It would never be just that way again, and they knew it. It was a golden moment on a golden autumn day in Moldova!

The Big White Truck

Moldova! What a wonderful mission experience! Nothing could ever equal that for me—it was my first mission trip, and I loved it. George had been to Haiti earlier in his life when he went there to install an X-ray room at the mission post located outside of Port-au-Prince. As I mentioned, George had formed a medical equipment business, and for use in this business he purchased a big, white Ford four-wheel drive truck. When we went overseas, we were to depart for Russia and beyond from Orlando, and that is where Bill and Sunshine Waters live. Bill consented to keeping George's truck while we were away, and George told him to use it if he needed it. And did he need it!

By this time Bill was a pastor in the Orlando area, and they were conducting an evangelistic campaign while we were on our trip to Moldova. One night at one of the presentations, a gentleman who had been attending the meetings night after night filled out an attendance card stating that he would like a visit from Bill. Bill gave the card to one of the members of his visitation team with the instruction to go find this man.

The team member drove all around the area where the man specified that he lived, but his house could not be found. The team member came back and told Bill that he couldn't find this address. Bill said, "He knows where he lives, and he wrote it down, so his address does exist. Please go and try again."

The team member went out again, but this time he stopped a mail carrier and asked him about this address. The mail carrier informed him that, "Yes, he does live down that particular road, but you will need a four-wheel drive vehicle to get there." (Can't you see the "wheels" turning in Bill's mind as he smiled knowing that he had George's big, white Ford truck at his disposal?) Bill told the team member, "Let's go. I have just the truck to get us there." And with that statement, off these two men went in search of this address. They found the road, and down its sandy ruts they went bouncing along until a house came in view just behind the tall hedgerow.

As the mail carrier had said, this house was the correct address, and the gentleman who had filled out the card was standing on the front porch waiting for them as he saw them approaching. With tears in his eyes he related the following: "Last night I had a dream. I dreamed that two Christian men would be coming to see me, and they would be driving a 'big, white truck.'" This story ended with this man and his wife completing Bible studies and becoming a part of the Seventh-day Adventist Church. Praise the Lord for how He uses all of us if we are committed and ready for service.

Chapter Six

Stateside Again!

All Around Florida with the Brownlows

Dr. Harmon Brownlow, at the time of our going with them to Moldova, had been in evangelism for many, many years. His wife, Margaret, had been on many of these campaigns after their children were grown. Sometime after we came back from overseas they asked George and me if we could travel with them for some crusades to be held in Florida. We really loved the Brownlows! They were committed Christians, and they were a lot of fun to be around. That's a very good combination to have when one is doing a lot of packing and unpacking. It also helps when traveling the roads in all kinds of weather—mainly hot sunshine and lots of rain at times when one is in Florida.

Once when we were traveling to Miami, we had trouble with one of the vehicles. That meant that George and Harmon had to leave Margaret and me alongside the highway while they went for help. It was midday, and it was hot! Margaret and I talked and drank lots of water while we waited. We tried to stand in the shade of our trailer, and that helped. Soon we saw the men approaching, and after repairs we were off to our destination. O, the perils of travel!

Going Around and Around in a Field

On one other trip to southern Florida, we ended the day by having to travel at night. For some reason we missed our exit and ended up in the Homestead area. If you can imagine this, please do! Harmon was pulling their trailer, and Margaret was driving their car right behind him. Next, there was George pulling our trailer with me driving our car behind him.

This caravan needed a place in which to turn around, so we went down a farm road and turned around in an empty field. I can assure you that my eyes were wide open with apprehension at that maneuver. Remember, I'm the caboose, and I had no idea where we were. But we made it to the church where we set up the campers and slept through the night before setting up equipment and supplies in the church. It was sometimes a challenge, but God was always with us, protecting us, and guiding us on our way. (Looking back, I have always wondered what the landowner must have thought when he surveyed all our tire tracks in his field. On our part it could have been classified as an emergency, couldn't it?)

At this point, I would like to enlighten most of you as to what an evangelistic crusade entails. You will be surprised as I was when I first realized all the details and plans that are involved. Imagine going with the Brownlows and the Garricks on an evangelistic "crusade" as they used to be called. Some people say "effort," and others use the word "campaign." We'll use crusade. Okay?

A Typical Crusade

So, I'll tell you how it was on a typical crusade. First, a hall had to be found and rented, and arrangements made for the services to be transferred to the specified church auditorium at mid-point in the meetings. Numerous letters were exchanged between Harmon and the pastor of the church of that particular city. (These days it would be more with a cell phone and e-mails.) Brochures had to be chosen and ordered and date of delivery specified for that area. (Later George would need to go to the different post offices in that town to make sure of the correct date received and brochures mailed on the right day.)

Volunteers were chosen as greeters, record keepers, nursery attendants, parking attendants, musicians for special music, pastor's role in the meetings, and many, many more items that had to be taken care of by the evangelist and his wife. Stationery, stamps, typing paper, and office supplies had to be on hand. The special gifts for attendance were ordered and received. George was on standby for whatever was needed from him. I had music lined up to play, and I was the videographer for the meetings.

The presentations were taped nightly, duplicated, and replayed the next evening before the service started. Many people have made decisions for the Lord from just seeing these replays. At times work schedules prevented some from attending the actual meeting and viewed the replays late morning with good results.

All Hands on Deck

When we arrived at the scheduled city, it was "all hands on deck." I have known the men to stay at the hall until 3:00 a.m. on most occasions of "setting up." The electrical wires and television cables are strung out and hooked into the proper outlets and mics. The stage is decorated extensively and beautifully for viewing enjoyment. My portable piano is set up along with the camera, switcher, and DVD recording unit. A switcher is a device that allowed me to go from the speaker to the screen for the scripture slides.

Follow Me, Please!

(When we started assisting the Waters Team, I was put in the position as videographer for the presentations each night, and thereafter, I did that for the other two teams in which we had a part. I learned the rhythm of Bill's approach to speaking as he walked slowly and taught at the same time. Dr. Brownlow's style was to mostly stand in the same spot as he proclaimed the Word. But with Ron Halvorsen it was a different story: His was a more animated approach as he moved back and forth. It was known that he had been a prize boxer in his youth, and these moves served him well in evangelism. Usually when he switched to the scripture slides, I could always tell by how he moved in that direction. And, of course, in later years when I did the filming for my husband, I found his movements familiar and easy to follow. They were all terrific speakers, and I wouldn't take anything for the experience of sitting at their feet each night, always learning new truths while actually filming them and their messages. There were times that I was so engrossed in what they were saying that I would momentarily forget to follow their moves.)

I'm back. Then the spotlight had to be placed in just the right spot and a person chosen for that duty. We arrived usually on Tuesday, and by opening night on Friday at 7 p.m. all was ready for the services to begin. There is always excitement in the air, especially on opening night. The questions arise: "Did we get the brochures out on time? Did the newspaper article reach people? Did our people invite their families and friends? What about parking?" The list goes on and on.

Finally the service begins, the Holy Spirit is present, the people have come, and God truly blesses the efforts that were put forth. I have left out many details, I'm sure; however, don't you just get the feel of evangelism and the excitement of winning souls for the Lord? The work has only begun for the team. The visitation teams go into action at the end of the second week. The evangelist's wife does the record keeping with her assistants. She also sends out at least three letters during the crusade which tell about upcoming presentations, gifts, special music, etc.

At the end of the crusade the baptismal candidates march out, and one by one they go into the baptismal pool, testifying to their new-found faith and their commitment to serve the Lord. They rise out of the waters of baptism into newness of life in the Lord. I always felt so blessed as I witnessed these services, then and now. I haven't kept count of how many hundreds that I saw go down into the waters of baptism; however, I know there were many. I distinctly remember how the deacons in one church helped a gentleman down into the pool by way of his sitting in a chair. That reminded me of the helpers in the Bible who took up roof tile and let down the afflicted one at the feet of Jesus.

Another time there was a lady who was deathly afraid of water and even had trouble in getting into her bathwater because of this inordinate fear that gripped her life. Before her scheduled baptism, the team at that moment anointed and prayed for her. With the Lord's help she was baptized and later exclaimed that she felt no fear at all of the water. What a release from that fear.

You may wonder how we managed to leave our homes and go on these crusades several times in a year. As I wrote previously, George owned a medical equipment business. This allowed him to schedule his time away and leave his assistant in charge. So this will be a brief insight into how we worked this out each time. We had to make all personal arrangements as to making sure the house was winterized, the bills paid, and, in our case, the animals cared for and the mail taken care of by a friend or neighbor.

The next thing was to get our living quarters (our fifth-wheel trailer) loaded and ready to go. George always gave me a difficult time concerning all the clothes and shoes that I managed to hide around in the camper. My philosophy was: "You never know what you will be doing or where you will be going, so take a lot, just in case." The gentlemen readers will relate to what George felt as he loaded these things in the camper. (I did manage to give him a little space in the closet.) Then the equipment trailer had to be gone through to make sure of supplies and equipment. Finally, with lots of effort, we had our vehicles filled with fuel and the trailers packed. Then we hooked on and off we went "on the road again."

Chapter Six

Elmer and Mabel

One of these crusades took the Brownlow Team into a city in central Florida. I will tell you that there has been an on-going controversy as to whether a church sign should be covered or left uncovered during a crusade. In this particular church, there was probably a question over this, but I remember that the sign was covered.

A rather distinguished gentleman and his wife, Elmer and Mable Barnes, started attending these meetings right from the start. They never asked what church— they just came night after night. (By the way, Elmer had been one of Billy Graham's assistants for some years.) About two weeks into the meetings, Harmon and George started going by the home of this couple to say "Hello" and to say how much their attendance at the meetings was appreciated.

Eventually the Sabbath was presented, and it was announced as to our denomination being Seventh-day Adventist. Elmer and Mable were doing a lot of soul searching as to what they should do in making a decision to start keeping the Sabbath and becoming a part of the Seventh-day Adventist Church. Finally, one night Elmer told Mable that if no one came by from the church before nine o'clock that night that they were going to take it as a "no" decision. That was his sign from the Lord, so to speak.

Elmer told Mable that if no one came by from the church before nine o'clock that night that they were going to take it as a "no" decision

In the meantime, Harmon and George were out and ended up in their neighborhood. Harmon looked at George and said, "Should we go see them tonight or shouldn't we? It is getting on toward nine, should we?"

George replied, "For some reason, I feel that we should go see them."

They went to the door, and they were invited in. After a few greetings were exchanged the question arose as to Elmer and Mable making a decision to be baptized and becoming a part of the Seventh-day Adventist Church. Their decision was to go ahead with baptism; however, before they left, Elmer told the ministers that he had made a stipulation for a decision and told them what it was. After hearing that, needless to say, the men were glad that they had made the decision to go visit these dear people that particular night before nine o'clock.

Elmer told the men that he and his wife had gone by the Adventist church for years and never realized what church it was. George asked Elmer would they have come to the meetings had the sign been uncovered. He replied that they would not have come. Do you think that perhaps God "blinded their eyes" for a time until that very meeting took place? I do. And especially do I feel that way until new people have a chance to hear and see the Sabbath truth presented. Today these wonderful friends are tremendous soul winners for the Lord. Evangelism pays!!

Miami Beach and Halloween in South Florida

At times there could be a lot of excitement for the team. Sometimes we dreamed up things to do to create a little diversion. One night on our scheduled day off, the four of us went to a "white tablecloth" restaurant over on the coast for dinner. We had had a very good meal, and I suppose blood sugars were at top form because we were in jovial moods.

As we left our restaurant, we went by another one (white tablecloth, too). On a whim, I "dared" Harmon and George to go in and ask the maître d' if he had any reservation for us. But I added, "Say it in a backwoods sort of way." Margaret started walking off. She knew what was coming. She said, "Oh, no, Charlotte. He'll do it!" I was sort of kidding; however, the thought of their going in there just plain "tickled me." Even as I write this, I find myself grinning as if it was just happening. No harm was done, and we all had a good laugh. The men said they asked the maître d' my question in the backwoods drawl, and they said no one even looked up from their meals. After they came back out, we sauntered on down the sidewalk just enjoying the warm evening and a full moon above us.

Cats!

On another night of our day off, we decided to drive over to Biscayne Bay and look around. There were several parks to visit and several marinas. We pulled into a parking space at this particular marina and got out to walk around. Cats were all over the place waiting for a handout from the fishermen as they came in for the night. We found out from the fishermen that lobster heads are poisonous for cats to eat, so those aren't given to them. People from town brought food out for these cats because their food supply was scarce when one considers the number running around. Cats everywhere!!

In south Florida at one of our large churches, we happened to be having a presentation on a Halloween night. The men were a little apprehensive about what could happen since it was a night out of the ordinary. At the close of the service, a young woman and man came inside and looked all around as if they were "casing out" the church for what they anticipated doing later, or so we thought. They went back out to a car, and we found out that they had knocked over the portable meeting signs. Harmon went over to the driver's side of the car, and with his deepest voice he said, "Get out of here, right now!" At that point, he hit the top of the door rather hard to give emphasis. You know, as a preacher does when he sometimes hits the pulpit for an effect. It worked. They left.

As all of this was taking place, the church people had all dispersed. The men decided that they would take turns standing watch that night. But Harmon soon came to our trailer door knocking and informing George that he wondered if someone could be in the church. His reasoning was that there was a car across the street, and that the driver was blinking his headlights off and on. This alarmed the men since the iron gate had been shut, and the alarm was on in the church. But they called the police just in case there was to be foul play.

Our campers were parked one in front of the other at the back of the church where the iron gate was in front of a double door. I lay across our bed on my stomach and put my chin on my folded arms for a ringside seat at the window. If there was to be action, I wanted a front-row spot, as they say.

The police came, and before the church door was unlocked, the policewoman shined her flashlight over our trailers. As she did, she saw just my head at the window with my "beady" eyes looking at her. George said very quickly, "Oh, that's just my wife looking out" He later told me that my eyes looked like "possum eyes" up there shining in the light from the flashlight. Another thing that he told me was that there was a gun pointing at me along with the flashlight. I'm glad that George was standing there to tell her who I was. He explained that those were our personal campers.

Just as they do on television, the police went inside, but they made George go first and turn off the alarm system. Then the police pushed open the doors as they came to them, and jumped aside (just as on television). After they checked out the church from one end to the other, they left. But the same young man and woman were going down the sidewalk, and the police stopped them for questioning. The woman was wanted on another charge and was taken in for further questioning. Halloween night in evangelism!

A Demon in the House

In another Florida location, George went to visit the husband of one of the church members who had been attending the seminar. He was away on an assignment at sea; however, his wife requested that George "visit her." She began to relate to George what had happened the night before as she lay sleeping. She said that she had been choked as if unseen hands were around her neck. She said that when she spoke the name of Jesus that the tension was less around her neck, and she was released. One of her children came to her crying and saying that something had held him down during the night. The mother asked George what could it be? George replied, "Sounds like a demon to me."

He asked her if she had any bad music in the house. There was none. It wasn't the best, but it wasn't "rock." George told her that there had to be something else in the house. She said, "Well, my husband does have a porno video in the closet, and I'll get it." The two of them decided that since it belonged to her husband that they shouldn't just throw it away; however, they did decide to remove it from the house to an old car in the back yard. George left their home to continue his visitation, but the next time that he saw this lady at the church she informed him that she hadn't had any more problems. He saw her again a year later, and she said that their home was demon free.

> *George replied, "Sounds like a demon to me."*

Keep on Keeping On

George and I appreciated the opportunity that we had in working with such an outstanding evangelist and his wife—the Brownlows! We learned so much from them. They were very tenacious, yet loving and kind. One has to have tenacity to "hang in there" when the going gets tough. Equipment sometimes will fail; the power can suddenly disappear; a thunderstorm can roar overhead, but as the worldly saying goes: "The Show Must Go On."

In our case, it wasn't a show. It is always the Lord's work, and we must go on. We've never missed an appointment for a meeting. I've been terribly ill at times, and I probably should have stayed in the camper. But, the people are there. The meetings have been advertised, and with a smile we just do what needs to be done. I've seen all the evangelists with whom we have worked go onstage very sick. George started a crusade in our later years with a temperature of 102 degrees. Perspiration was literally running off the end of his nose. The people were there, and somehow the Lord gave him strength.

One of the evangelists became ill with an upset stomach one night in the middle of a presentation. His wife just kept the pictures rolling until he could come back on after losing his supper outside. Sometimes, however, other arrangements do have to be made such as the case of a death of a family member or a car accident, etc. Once Bill and our team had to fill in for another evangelist when that evangelist became too ill to meet opening night. It just seemed to come together all right. But, it does make one nervous. With these memories, we'll never forget our wonderful and interesting times with these faithful men and women of God.

The Brownlows have a beautiful mountain retreat/home in the Blue Ridge Mountains of North Carolina Their home is just over the mountain ridges behind our home that we had at that time. We were able to visit and fellowship and attend the same congregation when we were at home between meetings. The Carolina Conference officers knew that we lived up there, and when Net '97 was planned, the Brownlows and the Garricks were asked to "lead out" in the preparations necessary for the Boone, North Carolina, site.

A most beautiful place was secured for these meetings in a conference building located on a high ridge at Appalachian State University. The brochures went sent out, and many precious people came each night for these presentations. As a result, much seed was sown, and many people came to the Lord and were subsequently baptized into the new company formed in that town.

The Horse Story

People have told us some funny stories over the years in our evangelism travels. In the Boone location a deputy sheriff attended the meetings every night, and after the services were over, he would stay by and tell us things that happened in his line of duty. His name was Robert, and he said on one dark night a call came in that two officers needed to go out into the country and check on a dangerous situation. He said that they went down this dirt road and cane to a place where they had to stop and go the rest of the way by foot. Their path took them by a mountain farmhouse. The time was midnight and dark! Very dark!

He said just as they crossed over this barbed wire fence the back-porch light came on, and a lady came out and hung up some laundry. The deputies "froze" until she went back inside. They continued their journey across this field, and he said that as he walked he felt a hot wind on his neck. When they got across to the next fence, he discovered a horse right behind him. This horse apparently walked all the way across the field breathing his hot breath down this deputy's neck. This story was so hilarious as Robert related it to us as to how he almost jumped out of his skin on seeing this horse's eyes in the light from their flashlight that dark night.

A 3ABN Encounter

I'm thinking of another story from this same area as the horse encounter. An amazing discovery was a lady who had been keeping the Sabbath for years after hearing about it on 3ABN. There was no church there, but she kept that day holy anyway. Tears flowed down her cheeks as she expressed her joy and delight at the prospect of having a church established in her area.

I'm happy to say that after the crusade, a church was organized and is prospering to this day. That church was the result of the joint efforts in this Net '97 crusade, and George and I felt privileged to be a part of this with the Brownlows. Praise the Lord! Robert, the deputy sheriff, is the head elder in this same church in Boone, North Carolina. Several new young couples were baptized, and they and their children became very important in establishing this work in this lovely university town in the Blue Ridge Mountains of North Carolina. A vibrant work had been done in the nearby areas of Banner Elk and Valle Crucis, North Carolina; however, with the establishment of a church in Boone a dream was realized. So many young people come and go through the halls of the university, and a work was finally begun to reach these students with the truth of the gospel as opposed to the New Age influence that we perceived was widespread in that little town.

The Brownlows have remained dear friends to George and me. I have fond memories of our time together in evangelism—the times of seeing people make the all-important decision of accepting Jesus as their Savior, and the decision to follow Him all the way into a new life of obedience to all His commandments.

Margaret Brownlow and I found the malls in the cities where we worked alongside our husbands. She and I had fun doing a lot of "looking" at the merchandise in these stores, and we knew where the sale racks were for our evangelism clothes when we needed them. We still keep in touch, and we pray for each other as we continue our individual journeys down the road of life.

Chapter Seven

This and That

For the most part, our experiences over the years have been positive. However, I tend to want to "tell it like it is." Once in a great while we could come up against a situation where personal feelings could come to the forefront. That is sad, but it is true. All of us are so human. Sometimes two personalities meet that aren't compatible. If there is a pastor who happens to be reading this part, please let me assure you that it is never the intent of the evangelistic team to come in and usurp your position. That pulpit is yours and well it should be. You have been called to that very spot. Evangelistic teams do what God and the local conference ask them to do, and that is spread the gospel.

I believe that more reassurance is in order at this point. For pastors, it may mean six weeks or so when you feel totally out-of-control of your church. Things are upside down, so to speak, and I don't blame you for feeling as you do when a team descends upon you and your staff. The evangelist and team need so many things done so that the meetings will be a success. The copier seems to run a lot, and that probably makes a pastor nervous. The piano is played a lot for practice. The building is open constantly, and I know you miss your privacy.

One special pastor was really overwhelmed at the thought that the evangelist at that moment in time had George as his assistant. The pastor wanted an assistant, too, and he told George, "Go take out this trash." (And the pastor had just met George, and we all were in conversation.) George sort of didn't hear the request and never took out that trash. We saw just plain human nature in that incident, and we smiled. It wasn't about the trash at all, was it?

So you see, the assistants on an evangelist's team are occasionally treated less than, and that is because people don't understand how it works. By that I mean that the assistants are usually business or professional people who can afford to take time to travel in the crusades and offer their expertise where needed. The evangelists never came across as feeling that we were less than. The truth is that they can't function well without some added help, and they value that help. The slights were rare for us.

In one place, the pastor was so anxious to get home at night that he almost was at the point of tears when the team and helpers lingered too long in their duties. He looked at me, and in a whining voice said, "Don't they know that I want to go home?" I just sort of shrugged my shoulders. After all, I was only an assistant, and it wasn't my job to hurry people. I realized that this pastor was physically tired and really did feel like going home to bed. These two incidents are minor, but they happen.

We all have to let the Lord give us patience in trying times like those. The evangelistic teams need to look at things from the perspective of the pastors and the members as well. The teams come in with time pushing them to be ready for opening night. When opening night comes, time waits for no one. You are "on."

> *We all have to let the Lord give us patience in trying times*

In Appreciation

Most of the time the team was always made to feel welcome. Many times we were entertained by different members of the church. A night out on a yacht, a meal at a famous restaurant, a fishing trip for the men, and shopping trips for the ladies. It all boils down to evangelism being the Lord's work, and we are just instruments in His hands. Evangelistic team member are so human too, and I know that they make social blunders as well as anyone else. Courtesy and kindness go a long way toward smooth relationships.

Humanity in Action

The reactions that we got from members were puzzling at times. As I said, we are all human, and we don't know how we would react if circumstances were the same. In one city in central Florida, a non-believing husband of one of the members started coming to the meetings. He became very interested in spiritual things, and he wanted to make some changes and start keeping the Sabbath. We were shocked to learn that his wife was very upset that he was making a decision for the Lord. She said, "Now I won't have anyone to go to the store for me on Saturdays."

Chicken?

At another large church toward the east coast of Florida, George approached a new regular attendee by the name of Linda about making a decision for following the Lord in baptism. Linda said, "I can't join your church. I eat chicken."

George said, "Who told you that you have to be a vegetarian to join the Seventh-day Adventist Church?" She said that the lady who sold vitamins told her that. (George and I are quick to tell people that the original diet is the best, but we don't condemn them if they eat clean meat. Actually, there is no condemnation from us.) The presentation in the seminar covers the subject of health and all aspects of that. All the evangelists went in depth into the study on our health message.

That night the vitamin lady came walking up to George, and in an irate way said, "Why did you tell Linda that she could eat chicken and join our church?"

George replied, "She can. Jesus ate meat."

This lady looked at George in all seriousness and said, "Well, Jesus didn't have Sister White back then." How would you answer something like that? I believe George just shook his head and walked off in disbelief. The truth is that new prospective church members are usually making decisions to become vegetarian. They do have the power of choice. However, the unclean things are pointed out, and they are expected to abide by what it says about that in Leviticus 11.

Things happen that can throw things "out of kilter" for the potluck committee. Such as the time when one of our new ladies brought a huge container of her very own fried chicken to potluck. The hostess came running to the evangelist, and in a frantic voice said, "Mrs.____ brought fried chicken to our potluck. What should we do?"

The evangelist replied, "Put the chicken on the table, and if any one of you eats chicken, then eat chicken!" We should never embarrass a new person or hurt their feelings. There was a time when I probably would

> *We should never embarrass a new person or hurt their feelings. There was a time when I probably would have reacted just as this hostess did with, "What should I do?" We should always do what Jesus would have done*

have reacted just as this hostess did with, "What should I do?" We should always do what Jesus would have done.

Punch, Anyone?

I heard another very amusing story concerning the beverage to be served at fellowship lunch at one church in South Carolina. Two of the church gentlemen were in charge of making their own special rendition of "punch." One of the new ladies brought a bottle of tomato juice and set it down among the other ingredients. Then she stood there just waiting to see what they were going to do. What would you have done? The two men looked at each other for one second with the question mark written on their foreheads, and then they opened the tomato juice and mixed it right in with the fruit juices. People said that it was the best punch the men had ever concocted. Do you think God smiled at that? I do.

First Impressions?

There is another area in which a lot of tact is needed, and I want to address that at this time because a whole lot of people don't know what's going on in the type of outfits that the evangelist wants his personnel to wear during the meetings. Some evangelists have resorted to having matching outfits made for the ladies who help in the area of greeters and record keepers. That only worked if certain sizes were available among the helpers. The outfits only went to size sixteen, and these days a lot of ladies are mature and over that size long ago. Then others have asked that all who help should wear black skirts and white blouses, and the men who help should wear dark slacks, a white shirt, and a tie.

At several places, we have been rather embarrassed at some of the attire that some have worn. It really matters to new people when they first come to the meetings, and the helpers are presenting themselves in the correct manner of dress. I remember at one meeting in a small church that one of the larger female volunteers came dressed in a T-shirt and skimpy shorts. We cringed, but we hesitated to say anything for fear of hurting her feelings. Evidently she had missed the planning session in which the correct dress code was emphasized.

I read of a study done on proper attire for different professions. They dressed several men in different styles and included one dressed in a dark suit. They then asked several people in a survey which one was the minister, etc. Each time the one dressed in the dark suit was named the minister. I have noticed that when I go to the mall dressed in nice clothes that I am treated better by the salespeople. Clothes do matter!

Years ago, we had an old model Cadillac which was comfortable for traveling around the country. Every time we stopped in for fuel, the attendant seemed to do a better job of cleaning the windshield and checking under the hood. (Remember those days?) Even though that car was old, he still recognized the name, and it made a difference in his mind. (That was back when one could get full service.) I'm telling you this because it is all part of evangelism. We are God's representatives here on this earth, and we want to be the best that we can be for Him. By the way, this is not to say that one has to have a very old Cadillac. It is just an illustration of how appearances do make a difference.

George in a Tuxedo?

When George and I started assisting evangelists, it was popular for the men to wear tuxedos. I remember our going to a store that sold used ones, and we bought one for the men to wear on stage for opening night. The shirt was ruffed, and the outfit was totally a novelty for George since he was a blue jeans or slacks man during the week, and a suit was for Sabbaths.

Somewhere there must be a picture of his wearing it. The tuxedo was black and the shirt was red. Get the picture?!

I remember Elder Cemer was wearing a white outfit at my baptism sixty-five years ago. Now the evangelists seem to mostly wear dark suits, and occasionally, a jacket, tie, and odd slacks for week nights. Always the tie. To this day I usually stress that George wear a tie. My reasoning is that if he wears one and gets to his destination and the other ministers aren't wearing a tie, then he can always take it off if he wishes. Sometimes he balks at the idea of the tie. (Confidentially, I wouldn't want to have one tied around my neck all day either, but such is the custom, isn't it??!)

Going to a Lot of Trouble

Now you have a glimpse of behind the scenes in evangelism. It seems that the evangelists go to a lot of "trouble," but that is why I suppose some have called it an effort. It is done in an effort to win souls. Jesus gave up heaven to come and dwell among us as the Great Evangelist. He certainly "went to a lot of trouble or effort." The study into why He did it has been the profound and mysterious subject for centuries. Even the angels desire to look into this theme; therefore, as much as possible, our energy must be directed toward the end of seeing people ready to meet Jesus when He comes back again. We will then have all of eternity to contemplate the reasons and whys of this life.

Is It a Secret?

There are many who have been taught that our Lord's return will be a secret event. There are many texts that say differently, and I will include a favorite at this point: 1 Thessalonians 4:16, 17: "For the Lord Himself will descend from heaven with a shout, with the voice of an archangel, and with the trumpet of God, and the dead in Christ will rise first. Then we who are alive and remain shall be caught up together with them in the clouds to meet the Lord in the air. And thus we shall always be with the Lord." This sounds exciting to me knowing that either way, we will hear the announcement of His coming. I surely want to be ready for that day and hour, don't you?

Come, Lord Jesus!

Consider one other text: Revelation 1:7: "Behold, He is coming with clouds, and every eye will see Him, and they also who pierced Him. And all the tribes of the earth will mourn because of Him. Even so, Amen." Plainly this says that every eye will see Him when He returns. That is such good news!

Of recent years I have found myself scanning the skies more and more. In our yearly visits to Arizona, I found that the skies over the desert are so beautiful because the vistas in some places give one a 360-degree view of the blue dome overhead. Many days the wind currents from California cause the clouds to separate into lacy and sometimes feathery patterns. I try to imagine the sky filled with angels when I see these formations.

I know that it will be so grand and awesome on that day when He comes. He is coming back because He Himself told us so in Matthew 24:30, 31: "Then the sign of the Son of Man will appear in heaven, and then all the tribes of the earth will mourn, and they will see the Son of Man coming on the clouds of heaven with power and great glory. And He will send His angels with a great sound of a trumpet, and they will gather together His elect from the four winds, from one end of heaven to the other." He invites us to accept His salvation which is the marvelous gift of eternal life in heaven with Him. John 3:16: "For God so loved the world that He gave His only begotten Son that whoever believes in Him should not perish but have everlasting life."

Chapter Eight

New Paths

On our very last meeting with Harmon and Margaret in central Florida, Ron and Carrol Halvorsen came by where we were staying and inquired about George assisting them in the upcoming annual field school of evangelism. For several years we had been attending the annual sessions of the evangelism council meetings held at the Hilton Hotel in Daytona Beach, Florida, and where George obtained his lay pastoral certificate prior to his ordination later on. These were conducted by Ron and Carrol during the times in which we attended. Many times it was my happy privilege to accompany the song service at the beginning of each session. George usually offered them his assistance in sound or in carrying in and out their supplies, etc. So, we were excited to be invited to assist with another aspect of Ron and Carrol's ministries.

Thousands have been thrilled at hearing Ron's testimony of his conversion in his presentations and in his book, *Gangs to God*. We have heard it many times as he moved his audiences with this story. His life is truly a miracle and a testimony to the mighty power of God in a person's life. It is also a profound argument for the existence of God. What else could explain this transformation in Ron's life and in all the lives of those who have accepted this gift of eternal life that Jesus offers to people everywhere? So it is understandable why we would be excited to have this opportunity to be of service to him and his wonderful wife, Carrol.

These field schools were sponsored by Southern Adventist University, and this one was to be held in Fort Myers, Florida. At that time Harmon had decided that he would take some time to think about whether to retire or keep on going. George and I were always mostly "freelance," so we decided to run home for a few weeks and then travel down and try out the field schools.

What a wonderful experience! There were ten ministerial students who came down to this one for an evangelistic crusade to learn and get college credit for attending the school. These young men were enthusiastic and very spiritual, but I could tell that they missed their wives and special people. Ron had a wonderful lady who came to these field schools to do the cooking for the students. Ruth was a seasoned camper and took all the "hardships" in stride. Her "boys" enjoyed her pampering them and catering to their food preferences. These young men occupied the rooms at the church school since the church school classes were over for the summer. Since I never went over there, I will tell you that George said they slept on the floor in their sleeping bags. For them, it was probably like going on a mission trip.

> *It is good to remember to pray for workers the world over; for, you see, it is a serious thing to go out and try to present truth to people, and it boils down to a life and death situation for them and for each of us as well*

These students were in Ron's classes each day, except Thursday, to learn evangelistic methods. George took the men with him some of the time for them to learn visitation skills. In addition to that, he taught them how to plan their day and how to efficiently map the city. Because of the marvel of computers, George had a mapping program that would let him place a house symbol over each address of a person of interest.

Ron Halvorsen was a powerful speaker for the Lord, and many thousands of people came to hear his Christ-centered presentations on salvation and prophecy. Always there were born-again experiences to awe and inspire us. Every time we knew there was a miracle in these conversions. Lives were changed. Sometimes the ministers had to go with converts to help set up their Sabbath work schedules.

Many people made lifestyle changes in giving up old habits. Very many felt the call to come out of Sunday-keeping churches. The majority of these dear people were already Christians, and when most people heard the truth, they seemed willing to accept it. But the ones who turned away from truth always stressed the teams. It is good to remember to pray for workers the world over; for, you see, it is a serious thing to go out and try to present truth to people, and it boils down to a life and death situation for them and for each of us as well. The thing that seems to keep evangelists going is the knowledge of the soon coming of Jesus.

Chapter Eight

Winds over Opryland and Beyond

One year the field school was held in Madison, Tennessee, which is just over the way from Nashville. The opening weekend was featured on 3ABN television, and Dr. Billy Burks was there with his marimba, and several other musicians such as Charles Haugabrooks performed before the presentation on opening night. Madison is such a part of our Adventist history, and I enjoyed being there in another history-making event as far as soul winning was concerned.

The Madison church, hospital, schools, and grounds are very beautiful in a rural-like setting. Our campers were parked one behind the other alongside one of the service buildings at the back of the campus. Our equipment trailer was first, then our camper, and last, Ron and Carrol's camper. Between us and the academy were magnificent old oak trees that were huge in circumference as well as in height. It was late spring, and the lawns were absolutely lush and green as the finest carpet in the world. It was also tornado season in Tennessee.

One night after a meeting, we had just come home to our campers and turned the television on to the weather station, and our weather radio was on for any emergency. The news was that there was a bad storm coming with a possible tornado in the area. We went to the Halvorsen's camper and alerted them to the danger, and we suggested that we all go to the church for safety. Ron had just gotten a newer truck, and he was especially concerned that it should not get hail damage.

All of us scrambled out of there, and we went into the church with our weather radios in our hands. We suggested to Ron that he park his truck under the portico. This he did and hurried into the church. Just then the weather news person in an excited voice exclaimed, "There's a tornado right over Opryland heading east." We started down the steps to the lower level, and as we went down, we heard a "bump" from up above the sanctuary level.

We had already had prayer for safety, and we were trying not to be afraid. We sort of huddled together on a bench at the bottom of the stairs and waited for the storm to pass. After it was over, we drove our vehicles back to survey the damage to our campers. There was none!! I repeat: There was no damage to our campers, but in front of our campers some of the huge oak trees were blown over, and limbs from the few that were still standing were scattered over the area. The next morning we discovered that the tornado did touch down over the church and did some damage to the roof. We drove through the neighborhood and saw the damage to many homes in the swath that the tornado had made through that part of town.

I have thought much about that night and tried to imagine what it would have been like to have been in our campers with the sound of trees and limbs being blown around like toothpicks. We were very thankful that God heard our prayers and spared our lives and our campers. We were thankful that the many buildings on campus were also spared intensive damage. By the way, Ron's red truck made it through the storm without a scratch!

Vocal Cords Repaired Here

If there is one thing that is of utmost importance to an evangelist, it would be his voice. By the time Ron Halvorsen came to Madison for an evangelistic campaign, he probably had spoken to thousands, perhaps millions, if one factors in his television and camp meeting appearances. What a terrific strain on his vocal cords. If one has to have repair on his vocal cords, then to be in the Nashville area would be ideal. Such was the case with Ron. Think of the speakers and musicians who live and work there.

The problem with his throat at that time was so severe that he couldn't complete the presentations before he had to have surgery for repair. Before his surgery he had gone to the surgeon for an evaluation. Ron was told not to talk, if possible. I remember going out of the trailer one afternoon, and there he sat by his steps with tape across his lips. He had such a great sense of humor, and that helped in what he was about to undergo. He had lived through the time of falling off the back of the stage at a crusade and having called for a friend to come up and help him. That was a funny story as he told it. And it caused a laugh when he related a time when his luggage was temporarily lost, and he had to stand up at an important meeting and preach in a jumpsuit. Now he needed those same attitudes as he prepared for this crucial surgery.

On the day of his scheduled surgery, he was asked to be at the hospital around 6:00 a.m. George and I were there with him and Carrol. Later, two of the church doctors came in to be with him during the preparation time before the surgery. After they took Ron in for his surgery, Carrol and the rest of us went to the waiting room to wait. In walked the students to be with her and to be there when the surgery was over.

In about two hours, word was sent down for Carrol to come up to the second floor for a conference with the surgeon. When she stood up, the rest of our group stood up. We all followed her up to the second floor for the conference with the surgeon, and when he walked through the door, his face showed that he was in shock at the number of people who were with Carrol. One of our doctors explained to him that these were Ron's students and that Carrol approved of their being there with her. With that knowledge, he didn't protest our being there but went on with his report of a good prognosis.

This particular surgeon is renowned for his skill in repairing vocal cords that are damaged through the years of stress and strain from public speaking or singing. Many of the Nashville "stars" who have needed surgical repair have sought after him for this skill. We could give God the glory for Ron being at the right place at the right time. As far as I know, he never had any more trouble with the vocal cords. And as an afterthought, Ron had a very nice singing voice.

These field schools were, as I said, an annual thing each spring at the close of the official school year at Southern Adventist University. Keep in mind that we continued to assist Ron and Carrol in these field schools for about ten years until he finally retired from that part of his ministry. We always kept that time slot open for these meeting in our schedule for each year. After the first one, we went home to check on the business and try to make some more money for our passion of evangelism. And our goats and llamas always seemed to be glad to see us each time that we came driving up our driveway. And I shouldn't leave out old, retired Dixie, the pet horse. She served her time as a farm/plow horse for a neighbor, and then we claimed her as our own for a pet and for grass consumption. "She eats like a horse!"

It was in the early part of this century that we were asked to do some interim pastoral/prophecy duties for the Carolina Conference of Seventh-day Adventists. We accepted and served at five or six churches in eastern North Carolina. This was a wonderful opportunity for us since it helped prepare us for what we would be doing in later years. The people were wonderful and kind in each of the churches where we were assigned, and we made many friends with whom we have kept in contact.

The Contract!

A major hurricane had come through the eastern part of North Carolina in 2000, and with it came destruction. We saw a lot of this left-behind devastation when we came into some of the little towns in that part of the state for a prophecy seminar. In evangelism, one never knows what awaits in the next assignment. George found a former bank building that was suitable for our meetings. It was unique, however, with the teller counter behind the pulpit and screens, etc. I had never suggested to George that he should get a contract on any previous buildings that we had rented. For some reason, I said, "George, perhaps you should get a contract signed before we begin meetings in this place." This was done and preparations were made. How glad we were for this piece of paper!

Always we put in the address of the auditorium in our brochures that were to be mailed out. That is what we did in Goldsboro, and when the governing committee of that bank building got their brochures, we were inundated with demands that we cancel our meetings. This building was to be the future home of the cultural center for the city, and the officials thought our brochure appeared to have their endorsement. This was not the case at all.

George called our conference president, and he said since we had a contract that we should go ahead with the meetings. The committee insisted that we not put our banner on the building. We were only permitted to put out a real-estate style sign each evening at the driveway entrances and remove them at the end of the service each night. I am revealing this to encourage other ministers to get that contract on the building if you are anticipating meetings. It saved the day for us.

This bank building was old, and the former occupants had moved to another location. We soon found out why. A terrible thing happened when water started pouring out from a stopped-up line at the street. To our credit, we helped clean up the place, and this was a great benefit to the cultural center. They thanked us profusely. George had an extra computer that he gave to the director, so troubled waters were smoothed, and we had a very good meeting.

Cats?

We needed a parking space for our camper, so we went looking for that. We went out on the edge of town and noticed that there were some mobile homes scattered among the trees. The area was wooded and weedy and looked like snake homes to me. But we went to the door of the owner's house and inquired as to parking somewhere on the grounds. Johnny Jones and his wife, Mary, were so kind to us. He said they really didn't have spaces at that time, but maybe they could find a spot in the very back.

Johnny and Mary had acres of abandoned greenhouses back there, and there was some plumbing and electricity available. He said, "Just pick a good spot and back in and set up." We did just that, but with my having many, many misgivings about the place. There were patches of waist-high grasses all around the area that spelled snakes for me. Not to worry! The cats had that taken care of! There were cats on every rooftop, on the fence posts, on the old vehicles, and under them.

An original set of cats had been brought in to control mice and other pests, and the cats inevitably multiplied. In the meantime, the greenhouses had been closed due to Mary's ill health, and the cats stayed. Johnny brought food out to them. (Just enough to keep them a little bit hungry for mice and snakes.) We made pictures of these beautiful felines as they wandered all about the place. We surely felt protected in such a unique setting with cats in the back and the owner in his house at the front of the property. God must have smiled at our "planned" circumstances.

> *We surely felt protected in such a unique setting with cats in the back and the owner in his house at the front of the property. God must have smiled at our "planned" circumstances*

There was a military base nearby, and every day the flight students lifted off in their jets flying just above the trees in our woods. When they reached a certain point in their climb, a whistling sound could be heard. We got used to that and hardly heard it after a while. Sadly one night Johnny and Mary's house caught fire. We never heard the fire sirens, and we didn't know about the fire until the next day when we drove out on our way to town. We were embarrassed that we hadn't been out to check on them. We were in a peaceful sleep and didn't hear the commotion.

As an Adventist, I found the city itself to be somewhat distasteful. That county is considered the hog-raising capital of the United States, so I was told by the residents. You can imagine the mantle of hog perfume that lay over that whole area. We tried to ignore this discomfort and concentrate on the mission at hand, and that was to see people give their hearts and lives to the Lord.

A Secret Revealed!

George approached his pastoral duties in an evangelistic way. One experience in the Greenville, North Carolina, church was one that involved a baptism. Chris, from one of the older families in the church, had decided to be baptized. His father, Ken, had put off being baptized for years, so George started encouraging him to also make a decision to be baptized when his son was.

No one else knew of the secret plans that were made by this father, his son, and George. The father had told George that if he had decided to be baptized after his son was baptized that he would have his robe on and walk out after he had baptized Chris. George walked down into the baptismal pool with the teenage son and baptized him. Then George announced that there would be one more candidate. Out walked Ken, the father, and the crowd came alive with joy. There was clapping, and there were enthusiastic, vocal praises that Ken had finally made his decision to follow the Lord all the way into baptism. That was a wonderful day for everyone.

George was like most every other associate who has worked with a well-known evangelist or evangelists for any length of time. Finally the associate has memorized the material and can easily do the presentations if necessary. George memorized Bill's material, and at Bill and Sunshine's encouragement and generosity in sharing their materials, George and I went solo in evangelism and pastoring after a few years of working with them and the other two couples.

We are greatly indebted to these wonderful husband and wife teams who mentored us over the years. They are people of God, and we learned so very much from them just by association if nothing else; however, there was in-depth training that took place. We were taken under their wings, so to speak. Under wings is a fine place to be, isn't it? There is shelter and protection there, and isn't it wonderful to know that there is another special place to be: "Under the wings of God." He invites us to dwell in that divine place of refuge.

So the next few years were spent in interim pastoring and gaining much experience with things that pertain to that calling. Though evangelism was still the passion for George and me, we did try to make George's ministry an evangelistic style which contained prophecy and doctrine. More than most people realize, the spouses play an important role in evangelism. The evangelist needs a lot of help in secretarial assistance. His clothes have to be laundered and pressed as well as dry cleaned when needed. An evangelist gets hungry all the time, so there are meals to prepare and dishes to be washed. And an evangelist can become discouraged at times, and that is when the wife can be an encourager even though she might also feel discouraged; however, she never tells him if she is.

Computers became such a blessing for the Lord's work. Over the years, George has perfected on his computer so many beautiful slides that he presents in his prophecy series. In most of the pastorates that he temporarily filled, George usually did a presentation of his program with slides. Many baptisms resulted from that emphasis. Not every person who attends church is necessarily a Christian or even an Adventist. These dear ones need to hear the gospel and given an opportunity to accept Christ and His teachings from His Word. Sabbath sermons have to be prepared for half who are already Christians, and half for the unconverted. Many times we have had people come forward whom the members just couldn't believe would ever make a decision. It pays never to give up on people. Ask and they will come if given an opportunity in the right setting. At least, that was our experience. For instance:

The Unexpected Conversion

Conversions make me think back to my girlhood days when we had a revival going in my "other church" before my becoming an Adventist. My father had attended church with our family all his time of being married to my mother. The pastors and the evangelists who would come to our church just assumed that Daddy was a Christian because he lived such a good moral life and attended church. The members knew that Daddy was not a Christian, but no one ever asked him if he would like to be.

One night during an especially good revival service, there was an altar call being given. I was seventeen at that time and a Christian. I felt very impressed to go back to my daddy and invite him to come forward and give his heart to the Lord. My father was a large man and very handsome, and I loved him dearly! There he stood with huge tears rolling down his cheeks, and he was holding tightly to the back of the bench in front of him. I gently took hold of his arm as he finally stepped out into the aisle, and I walked with him as he went forward to accept Jesus as his Savior.

There was not a dry eye in the church that night. I'm sad to say that within four months of his conversion, my father had a massive heart attack that took him away from our family and our church family and friends. The happy note is the fact that he had finally made a full surrender to the Lord when he did. Now you know why I was impressed to go back and lead him to that altar of surrender. I'll surely be looking for him and others when Jesus comes back again.

Chapter Nine

Trails West

For several years my older sister, Ruth, and youngest brother, Kelly, and their families had been living in Arizona, and it was through their eyes that George and I had come to love Arizona. Between meetings back east, we would many times head out there to enjoy the mild winters and visit with them. Kelly and Ruth accompanied us to the magnificent Grand Canyon, colorful and serene Sedona, captivating Walnut Canyon, mysterious Petrified Forest, and a couple of times we went up to Crown King, an old mining community of long ago. Crown King is in the Bradshaw Mountains of Arizona high above the valley floor of Phoenix, and to go there one must ascend over switchback roads that finally give way to a former railroad bed that substitutes for a road. And people ask us why we love Arizona?!

My brother, Kelly, had staked out several mining sites in the Bradshaw Mountains, and it was such fun going up there to camp and enjoy food and fellowship. Unknown to us, we were slowly being conditioned for some decisions that we would later make for a whole new way of life.

In the meantime, we were busy during the rest of the year with our crusades held in North and South Carolina, Florida, Alabama, Mississippi, Tennessee, and Virginia. Evangelists travel and minister under the names that are given for their own endeavors. George and I chose the name "The Light of Prophecy" for his ministry. Our medical equipment business was by then more of an avocation, and the business was mostly done by phone in taking orders from established accounts. Then, it was a matter of making the deliveries and setting up the equipment in the veterinarians' offices that we served. The reason I'm saying all of this is to let you know that this arrangement was ideal in that it gave us the options of when and where we could do a crusade. We were still "freelance."

Wachula

Our very first solo crusade in Florida was held in the little Adventist church in the small farming town of Wachula, Florida. We'll always be grateful for

Wachula. The pastor and the members were so very receptive and kind to us and non-judgmental. Wasn't that nice? The attendance was good, and we enjoyed our time there among God's people in that wonderful place. Several new people came to the meetings throughout the time that we were there.

While we were in Wachula a very funny thing happened down at the laundromat. Evangelistic teams usually have to rely on commercial facilities for personal laundry. The only time that I remember washing our clothes in a home was when we were in Moldova, and that was with very primitive conditions and a 220 power source. Scary! But this one time I remember so well because of my friend, the frog.

Apparently froggie got mixed up with a batch of our soiled clothes and made it through the entire wash cycle which included some laundry sanitizer. Just as the last spin cycle came to an abrupt stop, I happened to be there to open the lid, and out jumped the frog all creamy and white. For a moment he sat there in a daze as he looked up to me as if to say, "What are you doing? Are you trying to kill me?" It was at once comical with that little guy just sitting there, and also I felt terrible about his ordeal. It must have been quite a ride when the clothes monster started to spin—a rollercoaster? Even George thought it was funny because he is the one who suggested that I tell my readers about it.

Haines City

We went to Haines City Adventist Church from Wachula, and again, we were made to feel so welcome by our new friends there. The members were in the midst of scrubbing the church from top to bottom when we arrived. Unknown to us, there was a bit of resistance from the leader of the small religious college in that town. Several of their students were in attendance on opening night, and one of their students came over at some point and made a picture of our banner which was covering the church sign. In the article that he ran in the newspaper, which included the picture, he accused our people of being deceptive. All one can do then is to keep going in the name of the Lord and do the best that can be done. We were blessed, and I feel that the people were, also. I remember on closing night that one of the church gentlemen presented me with a huge bouquet of flowers as a gift from the members.

These dear members had a special interest in the children who attended Sabbath School and church services there. Each week there was a meal for the children and any adults who wished to participate in this provision of food. I loved the fellowship!

That was back in the early part of this new century, and I can't remember the exact number of baptisms. The other good news was that we were able to work hard on updating our slides and adding new ones as the world and local news changed. What a time to have been living. We felt surely that the Lord would come soon!

"Soup, Anyone?"

We traveled on up the coast of Florida into Alabama and Mississippi. It was hot and dry in those states, but we enjoyed our time there. Always there were interesting experiences for us. In one particular meeting, an older gentleman was having a hard time making a decision to be baptized. He was a very good Christian who belonged to another faith. His wife, however, had been an Adventist for a long time, and she was hoping that he would make a decision during our campaign that was held at the county fairgrounds.

As George and the pastor were traveling down the road to Calvin and Carrie's house, the pastor asked George, "Where are you going?"

George told him, "To Calvin's house." The pastor said that it wouldn't do any good. He said that two other evangelists had been there, and Calvin wouldn't make a positive decision for church membership. George grinned at the pastor and replied, "He hasn't told me 'no.'"

Carrie came to the door and escorted the ministers in. Calvin was sitting at the dining table eating some of her homemade vegetable-beef soup. Calvin said, "I would offer both of you some supper, but I know you wouldn't eat it. It has beef in it."

George replied, "Carrie, we're going to eat with Calvin. Dip us up some of that good-smelling soup." As she was a long-time Adventist, George knew that she wouldn't have put any unclean thing in the soup. He had already told the pastor to" eat around what you don't want." The men sat together and enjoyed a good meal along with some good-natured kidding. Tears were running down the side of Calvin's face in rivulets as the men fellowshipped with him over a bowl of soup.

Calvin later made his crucial decision to be baptized, and he told the ministers, "The fact that you ministers ate supper with me that night made a whole lot of difference to me in making my decision." I believe that Jesus would have sat down with Calvin if He had been the invited Guest, don't you?

Sky Writing?

At the close of one of the campaigns, George was asked by the conference to stay by for a couple of months for some Bible work among the members in that area. There were a lot of missing members, and George's assignment was to find all that he could and be of an encouragement to them in coming back to church.

On one of his visits, he discovered an address way "out back" that would need a "four-wheeler" to access this remote home. So he came back to our camper and asked me if I would accompany him out to this place in our truck. When we came bumping into the yard, the owner came out to greet us with a very puzzled look on his face. He asked George, "How in the world did you find me? No one else can find me!" George just smiled broadly and pointed up to the sky. That produced another look of surprise on this man's face. As you may have guessed by now, George had a mapping program in the vehicle that he was using, and that technology was so new that this man wasn't even aware of it. I don't think George ever told him that he had it because the man didn't ask more.

Bernie Pounds

While we were working in and around Mississippi, we were put in contact with a prisoner serving a ten-year sentence in the federal prison in Yazoo City, Mississippi. The story that we got was that Bernie found a Seventh-day Adventist tract lying on the floor of the prison, and he sent away for the Bible lessons that were offered in it. Bernie always felt that an angel must have dropped that tract there in prison for him to find. We never questioned that. We did make two or three visits to him in that facility. How I wish that all of the young people could visit such a place and see what could await an offender there. Visitors can't take anything into the facility with them when they go in to visit someone, and their car keys are even checked into the care of the receptionist at the front desk.

Razor Wire

At the appointed time, the visitors are escorted back to another area where they must leave their thumbprint in ink and have the back of the hand stamped. When that is done, then visitors are escorted through some huge doors out onto a walkway that connects these two buildings.

Encircling the buildings is the razor wire that puts fear in one's heart at the sight of it. And it can be very scary to hear the doors clang behind as you walk on toward another set of doors that will open and shut for you. As one enters the visitors' area, the attitude is one of concession to their rules and regulations. On one of our visits, one of the guards came over to us and made us move from the seats in which we were sitting. We never understood why. We just moved without saying a word.

On our first visit I remember that suddenly, another set of doors opened in front of us as we were waiting, and Bernie appeared. He recognized us from the picture that we had sent to him. He hugged us warmly, and the visit began. We have always taken to heart what Jesus said about "being in prison and you visited me." (We have visited other prisons in other times such as when George visited someone in a Moldovan prison.) One must remember that there is not much to talk about to a prisoner in the way of small talk since their horizons are so limited. We could, however, talk to Bernie about the love of Jesus and about our love and concern for him.

> *One must remember that there is not much to talk about to a prisoner in the way of small talk since their horizons are so limited. We could, however, talk to Bernie about the love of Jesus and about our love and concern for him*

I had written a book about our missionary travels overseas, and I had sent him a copy through the mail. Bernie became very excited about the prospect of his writing a book about his experiences in prison. He was an Adventist at that time, and he began to give Bible studies to any person who would listen. After his conversion, Bernie was given permission to be baptized by a lay minister who had been studying with him. You must know that Bernie is at least six feet tall and over, and to fit his frame into a laundry tub would seem impossible. But somehow, he reduced himself into that tub and was covered with the water of baptism. God looks on the intent of the heart and takes into account one's situation in life.

Bernie also taught some high school classes in prison, so, he was bright and intelligent. The material that he sent to me for manuscript preparation was in the way of explaining Bible passages, and he would tell me about situations that happened from day to day in prison. This was a federal prison, as I said, and on one of our visits he pointed out a judge who was serving time for some offense. I was always a little nervous about the prospect of being so close to individuals who were there because of violent crimes.

We had to remember why we were there, and that was to bring the knowledge of a forgiving Savior to these men through Bernie. (Prison evangelism and ministry.) We were able to bring many Bibles to this facility. We had meant for them to be used by Bernie in his Bible studies; however, the officials took them and placed them where they wanted them to be which was in the common area. This distressed Bernie very much.

Over the months from the time that we became acquainted with him, he began to keep letters coming to us. He would send pages of manuscript for me to type for him. Then suddenly, he stopped writing his book. He was very humble, and he was afraid that he would somehow dishonor the Lord by thinking himself capable of writing this book. Thereafter, I took his letters and finished his book for him just from stories that he wrote of what was happening in prison.

The conditions were bad for him. When one of the inmates disobeyed or caused an uprising, the entire prison population was punished as a consequence. Adequate food was withheld from the men. On one occasion of withheld food, the situation went on for some time, and a sympathizer made it known to some higher up authorities. These people sent word to feed the men. Bernie said that the men rushed to the tables and started eating like dogs because of being so near starvation. That hurt, I know. But everything that Bernie would relay to me, I put it into his book. After his time was served, a very close Adventist friend of his had this little book printed and distributed for him. George and I were able to give him a computer and a printer, and we saw that he was cared for by relatives. We hope to see him again when Jesus comes back!

Hindrances?

In one of our crusades in a small town "down south," we were up against a new thing. We were going to hold our meetings in an old storefront, and it needed some repairs and extensive cleaning. (Storefronts can be used very effectively in evangelism. They are everywhere in every city.) We were promised by one of the members that this place would be nice and clean and ready for us when we arrived. It wasn't. We had to start setting up anyway under less than ideal circumstances; we were under a time schedule for opening night, and we had to get our equipment set up.

The pastor told this person to please let us work in the way that we were accustomed to by getting the place cleaned as promised. This person couldn't understand why it needed to be done so soon and began further delaying the process of setting up. We were forced to go ahead and clean and dress up the place as best we could. This delay became a hindrance, and if you are familiar with the ways of an evangelist, you will understand why it caused us such dismay. We knew that this person didn't realize why this was so important to us, and we tried not to make "a big deal" out of it, but it had to be dealt with in some way.

We went to our knees and asked the Lord to take charge of this situation. I can't tell you for sure if it was His doing, but I can sadly tell you that this person became ill with influenza, and we didn't see that person again until near the end of the meetings We saw an altogether different attitude at that time. I feel that the Lord will fight our battles if we will let Him. We didn't stop loving this person, but we were disappointed and confused for a time.

A Hurting Heart!

It is said that every person has a story. Some are happy stories; some are sad. This particular one was one of the most distressing that I have every heard, even the ones on "Doctor Phil." One afternoon a very tearful, young woman asked that we listen to her account of childhood abuse at the hands of her father. We were scheduled to go to a planned wedding, but we had to cancel those plans.

It is said that every person has a story. Some are happy stories; some are sad. This particular one was one of the most distressing that I have every heard

This lady began by telling us that her father forced her to have sex with him on numerous occasions, and sometimes he held a gun to her if she resisted. Such crying and sobbing that came forth from her innermost self! George and I aren't trained as counselors as such, and we called the pastor in at her permission. He felt that she should be put in touch with a local counselor, and that was arranged. The very person who should have been her protector was her tormentor. A sad aspect of this case was the fact that this man was the head deacon in his church, and when I first arrived at that church a few weeks earlier, he was the one who threw his arms around me in greeting, and he didn't even know me. Perhaps he had made it right between himself and the Lord; however, we felt that there had to be a whole lot of healing between him and his daughter from that point forward. Satan is hard at work everywhere, it seems.

Breaking North Carolina Ties

After meandering around "down south" in several crusades, we headed back to the hills of home. We had built a smaller home, but we were away so much of the time that we never really bonded with that house enough to call it home. This house was far up on the side of a mountain, and when George was away, I was terribly afraid. I never expressed these fears to him that much, but it was just so remote. George said that I was probably safer there than I would have been in a city. I don't know about that. Listen to the following:

An Unwanted Guest!!

One morning as I came through my little anteroom/office to our bedroom, I saw a snake under my office chair. I called him "long tail" because I surmised that he thought he was hidden; however, a large part of him was extending beyond the back of my chair. I reacted very quickly and ran in and shut our bedroom door. I called down to 911, and the dispatcher said they would send someone to take care of my "visitor." A neighbor gentleman heard all of this on his CB radio, and he volunteered to come up and see about me.

When he came in through the bedroom window, he would crack open the door just a bit and peek in and jump back which let me know right away that he wasn't going to be successful in running out the visitor. I said, "Mr. Bauguess, don't you think that we had better call Harold to come up?" He quickly agreed. (Harold was his son-in-law.) Harold also came in through the window because I wasn't about to go back by the snake to the front door to let anyone in. So, the window.

Harold had installed the carpet in our house, and he didn't want to "mess it up with a snake." So he brought in a hoe through the window, put it in front of the snake who wrapped around it, and Harold excitedly told Mr. Bauguess and me, "Where are you? I'm coming through with the snake?"

I yelled back, "Where do you want us?" At that I'm sitting back on the bed with my feet up off the floor, and his daddy-in-law was in a chair, I think. Harold came through with the snake and out onto the deck, and down into the grass went "Long Tail." I survived! And we didn't have any mice running around after that.

Intruders

I remember that once when we were away in a meeting that our little house was burglarized, and two of my musical instruments were stolen—an old violin and a dulcimer. We did most of our own detective work and found the criminals; but, as it would be, they would never tell us who had my instruments. Our insurance company reimbursed us for the costs of them, but I missed them and the sentimental value that I placed on them. The dulcimer had been hand designed for me by Russell Sturgill, a now-deceased friend. These thieves were young men from the neighborhood, and we tried to talk to them about the spiritual aspect of their lives in relation to this felony. The judge apparently chose to order them to make restitution, pay their fines and court costs, and just let them go.

I hope what I am about to say will be understood as I mean it. After this break-in the spirits of the burglars remained in our house. Not that I could see anything, but I knew our privacy had been breached, and the house was never the same again. I think that is the most horrific part of an act such as invading someone else's space. I knew that every drawer had been opened, every cabinet had been looked into, and rusty hands had touched my personal things. The one consolation to all of this was the fact that because we had limited closet space, I had stacked quilts on the carpeted floor on each side of the guest room walk-in closet. In and among those quilts were the rest of my instruments such as a guitar, a mandolin, and a Russian balalaika. The little monster thieves thought they were just looking at quilts in this case. Wasn't I smart? I should have also put the others there. My dulcimer that was stolen was hanging on the wall in the living room.

Because of the aforementioned incident, it was not hard for us to decide to consider the west as a new destination. We were "ruined" anyway from traveling so much. How could we settle down in one spot with this wandering blood in our veins? The first frost had come, and the usual snowfalls were being anticipated by us; we decided to head back to Arizona. This house would remain as it was for two years while we were in Arizona in a new endeavor.

Chapter Ten

To the Mountain and Back

My darling sister, Ruth, passed away in 1995; however, the youngest brother, Kelly, and his wife, Beverly, still lived in the Phoenix area. Our custom was to park our camper in a park in Wickenburg and still be near our relatives. We had left North Carolina for the winter, and soon after our arrival in Arizona around the year 2003, George had contact with the president of the Arizona Conference of Seventh-day Adventists, and he invited George and me to travel to the Springerville, Arizona, church to see what we thought about working in that district as a pastoral team.

On arrival at the Springerville church, we looked it over and formed some definite opinions as to what we should do. The church was in a very remote part of the state. Ask anyone who ever traveled to Springerville from Phoenix, and they will tell you that it seems as though you'll never get there. It is remote!

The church proper was old and in need of repairs. The new sanctuary, which consisted of four walls with brown paper over the windows, definitely had the word "work" written all over it. Little did we know the real truth about all that was involved when we made our decision to go there. George reminds me that I said, "It looks like they need some help." Once again, we hooked up the camper to the truck, and off we went to conquer the city of Springerville and surroundings. (We even made plans for a crusade there.) Following George, who was pulling the camper, was "little ole me," and I was struggling to drive with a terrible wind forcing us one way and then the other. Obviously, we made it to the church where we parked and worked for the next two years.

Springerville is located in the beautiful White Mountains in the northeast corner of Arizona. Someone aptly named Springerville as the windiest city in the United States, and at times I felt that to be true. Sometimes the wind came in over the volcanic hills with such force that it was difficult to hold our car door open to get inside without a struggle.

The earliest settlers in the region were from Mexico and Spain, and in increasing numbers the early Mormon settlers came and became the majority in this frontier town. George and I found friendship among the Mormon people in Springerville and in the adjacent towns of Eagar and St. Johns. During our time in Springerville, it was George's happy privilege to baptize several Mormon friends into the Adventist church there. They proved to be happy and caring members.

The members of the Springerville church were wonderful. When they saw construction being started in earnest, they rolled up their sleeves and began to help George and me in the finishing of their little church. The Ken Ball family from back east who had moved to Phoenix came up on two occasions and directed the installation of the wallboard. (Remember? He was the surprise baptismal candidate in an earlier story.) As a team of workers, we tore down walls, we helped put up wallboard, we painted, we scrubbed, curtains were made, new flags were installed, new carpet was laid, beautiful blue pew chairs were placed in rows, and in general, it came together in one grand design. It sits now as a beautiful monument to the glory of God. Clark Roan of Roan Trucking Company graciously picked up the carpet and pew chairs and delivered them right to the door of the church and on inside of the building. Wasn't that a wonderful gift from such a generous company?

Because of the improvements to the church and grounds, the City of Springerville voted the Adventist Church as one of the recipients of the "Annual Beautification Award."

The finishing touch was the landscaping which became a full reality just after George and I had to move back down off the mountain. Because of the improvements to the church and grounds, the City of Springerville voted the Adventist Church as one of the recipients of the "Annual Beautification Award." We traveled back to Springerville where George and the pastor, Clarence Philpott (now deceased), accepted the award on behalf of the church. God has a way of remembering the efforts of those who choose to serve Him. We will always love these dear members of the Springerville, Arizona, Seventh-day Adventist Church.

St. Johns, Arizona

As I said, we parked our camper (a fifth wheel and roomy) beside the Springerville church. That was fine as long as the weather was permissible, and that was convenient for us in working inside the sanctuary. It started getting really cold by September, and we knew that we would somehow need to rent winter quarters. We found a home in St. Johns, thirty miles away, that was suitable. The owner was an elderly lady who was confined to a nursing home in Phoenix, and her brother made it possible for us to stay in this furnished home for the winter months.

St. Johns is predominately Mormon, and George and I felt that some of them were not too happy about our living in their town. One night as we were leaving Springerville to go to St. Johns and home, a red truck came up beside us and tried to run us off the highway. There was not another vehicle in sight for miles, so traffic was not the problem. He roared on past us, and we continued our journey.

Unwanted!

One day as I was working at George's desk in front of the side window, I thought I saw someone go by the window, and I jumped up to peer out to see who was going down our driveway. I told him what I saw, and he said, "I know what you are saying. I have seen the same thing many times, and there is no one out there." We lived there; so I decided to just keep observing and making mental notes. This house had a strange atmosphere to it; on the other hand, we had our Bibles with us, and we had our prayer life each day. So life went on with study, working, going to church....

One night and early in the morning about 4:00 a.m. as I was awake and just lying there waiting for the dawn, I experienced a strange occurrence. Suddenly, the opposite wall from the windows lit up, and a figure came swooping down and stopped right by my side of the bed. It was almost elf-like in appearance, and he was bent over and smiling down into my face. I murmured under my breath to George, "Did you see that?" He said that he didn't, and I told him what had just happened.

Before we slept in that house again, we took a Bible and opened it to the 91st Psalm and proceeded to start in the bathroom by our room and work our way through the house. We even went into closets and out onto the back porch. As we walked, we were saying out loud, "In the name of Jesus, get out of this house. We don't want you here. Get out, in the name of Jesus." When we got to the front door, we opened it and demanded that the "intruder/intruders" go out the door. We closed the door, and in faith believing that God heard our prayer, we never saw or felt any other strange phenomenon again. The name of Jesus is powerful, and the devils tremble!

The Fire

We are not sure what "lurked" around on the outside of this dwelling. After we left that house and that area, the next pastor moved in. At a later date he did some burning of brush in the back yard, then he went into the house, sat down in his rocking chair, and went to sleep. Soon he was awakened by a loud rap at the door and a neighbor's voice yelling, "Get out! Get out! Your house is on fire!" Apparently some embers that were still hot caught fire to the underneath part of the house, and it was a total loss except for a few household items that were saved. George and I have our own feelings about that house and yard.

A Change of Direction

If you remember now, I told you in an earlier chapter about my having a bout with cancer in 1987 with the side effects of chemotherapy and radiation. I had asked my radiologist about the damage that I thought was being done to surrounding areas of my body at the time of my treatments. He had said, "We'll worry about that later." Well, "later" had come while we were working in Springerville. The treatments had left me with a subclavian artery blockage that showed up with symptoms while we were working on the church. Also, the rotator cuff in my left shoulder was torn beyond repair, and that was probably the result of these same treatments received for the carcinoma under my left arm back in 1987. God had been so good to allow me to live and serve Him in my small way. But the pain and discomfort had become so bad. The doctors had agreed that a lower altitude would be recommended in my situation.

San Bernardino, California

While all of this was happening, George had made a commitment to assist Ron and Carrol Halvorsen with a planned crusade in San Bernardino, California, in October and November of 2003, and we were not going to let them down by not helping them. So we loaded up the camper and the car and off we went in search of some more souls who were also searching for truth. Once again, I was to be the videographer for this crusade.

My arm was hurting in an excruciating way, but I didn't let on to anyone about it. I had a long handle attached to the camera which was sitting on a tripod. Then I had a switcher at my left (hurting) arm and another piece of equipment with a cassette in it to record the meeting each night. So I was very busy operating these pieces of equipment. Our daughter, Renata, who is a nurse at Loma Linda Medical Center, came to our meetings, and we spent a lot of time together. She later said, "Mother, I am a nurse. How did you keep this pain from my knowing it?"

I learned in evangelism long ago that one does what one needs to do without too much complaining. God was looking after me, as they say, and in time, help was provided. In the meantime, this crusade was conducted with some exciting results. There were four hundred plus people who were baptized, and a local swimming pool had to be used for baptisms because of the multitude of candidates and guests.

These meetings were held at the famous "National Orange Show Event Center" auditorium each night, and usually it was near capacity at each presentation. Ron always had a way of delighting his audiences with funny quips regarding life itself, and at the same time, the messages were anointed and delivered to the hearts of the listeners. Even old-time Adventists were blessed to hear our messages again and again. Me included.

A Life Taken

From the beginning of this meeting at the Orange Show Auditorium there was a group of young men who were attending every night, and there was a question about whether these men were having fellowship with a local drug ring. Our people never said a word, but just waited to see.

One of the young men in this group showed much interest in learning more and more truths from God's Word. About the fourth week of the crusade, George visited with this man after one of the presentations, and he expressed a desire to accept Jesus as his Savior. He also asked about baptism and continued Bible studies. A drastic turn-of-events forever changed that decision, but it was recorded in heaven.

The meetings were coming to an end, and a baptismal service was to be held on the Sunday after the last service. This young man was scheduled to be among those to be baptized; but he failed to show up at the last Friday night's service. George and some men went to see what was going on, and they discovered that someone came to his home and shot him with his wife at his side. I can't imagine the horror of a situation like that, can you? What was the family to do at that moment?

As usual, this little family had no money and needed help. We understood that one of the very kind doctors at a nearby hospital had an extra gravesite and gave that for this man's interment. You can imagine the sadness that swept over the evangelist, his staff, and the audience. Our consolation was that this young man had made a decision to follow Jesus, and that was acknowledged in heaven.

When we finished the crusade with Ron Halvorsen in San Bernardino, we brought our camper back to Springerville; however, we felt our time was running out up there. Springerville is located at near 7,000 feet elevation, and because of my increasing health problems, we had made our decision to leave Springerville and head down to a lower destination. Our camper was parked beside the church while we were there.

In June we went to the Arizona Camp Meeting, and a decision was made for our going to the Wickenburg, Arizona, Seventh-day Adventist Church. When we got back from camp meeting, two of our Springerville ladies noticed that we didn't bring our camper back to the church. They quietly said, "You are planning to leave us, aren't you? You didn't bring your camper back." (We had taken our camper to Wickenburg and parked it in our usual RV park.) We just smiled; however, on that next Sabbath we gave the announcement that we had made the decision to return to the Wickenburg area in a lower altitude.

The shock was felt across the audience as the news sank in; for you see, we had made some very tight friendships with these lovely people in that remote part of Arizona. We knew that parting would be hard to do. On our last Sabbath with these friends, they had George and me come up front and sit in two chairs facing the audience. Then a group stood on the platform to sing a song for us. Many tears were flowing that day as we were presented with gifts and cards. Then we had our last fellowship meal with them on that very last Sabbath together. Heaven will be so wonderful when we can once again be together and never have to say good-bye. Several of these faithful ones have been laid to rest as I write on this day.

> *Heaven will be so wonderful when we can once again be together and never have to say good-bye*

I take great comfort in knowing about the promise of that resurrection day spoken of in 1 Thessalonians 4:13–18: "But I would not have you to be ignorant, brethren, concerning them which are asleep, that ye sorrow not, even as others which have no hope. For if we believe that Jesus died and rose again, even so them also which sleep in Jesus will God bring with him. For this we say unto you by the word of the Lord, that we which are alive and remain unto the coming of the Lord shall not prevent them which are asleep. For the Lord himself shall descend from heaven with a shout, with the voice of the archangel, and with the trump of God: and the dead in Christ shall rise first: Then we which are alive and remain shall be caught up together with them in the clouds, to meet the Lord in the air: and so shall we ever be with the Lord. Wherefore comfort one another with these words."

(Before we leave Springerville, I want to tell you about a delightful experience that happened in the White Mountains above Springerville, Arizona. It was a Sabbath afternoon, and we had guests from Wickenburg, Arizona. We decided to take a drive into these mountains to enjoy a bit of nature as a reprieve from the heat for our friends from down in the valley.

Suddenly as we rounded a curve on a dirt road winding its way around the hills, there were at least one thousand sheep lying peacefully on the ground around a little camper. One lonely shepherd and his sheep dog were watching over these special wooly animals. We stopped, and the shepherd came out and greeted us in Spanish.

This young man was from Peru, and each summer he traveled to these White Mountains to care for sheep during the summer months. He told us that he had a family and that he sent money back home to them. In a lot of sign language he invited us into his little camper and proceeded to make us some tea. We thoroughly enjoyed that afternoon adventure.

But that visit didn't stop at that point. Later we took a Spanish-speaking church member back up there with a Spanish Bible and some Spanish literature for his reading and studying. George and I went up there several times, and the last visit was out to where they were shearing the sheep. We told him we were leaving the area, and we wouldn't see him again. He gave us his address in Peru, and we said goodbye. We did take him his lunch for that day which produced a big smile across his beautiful, rugged, tan face. I fully expect to see this person in heaven someday.

After the summer months, these sheep are driven down the "Rim" (Mogollon Rim) to points down in the valley around the Phoenix area for their winter months at rest.)

Chapter Eleven

What About Wickenburg?

Years ago when George and I started going to Phoenix to see relatives, we usually ventured "out Wickenburg Way" as the saying goes. A nice A-frame Seventh-day Adventist Church was built around fifty years ago, and there have been additions made to this original structure along the way. We loved Wickenburg right from the start.

Wickenburg was named after Prospector Henry Wickenburg who came to Arizona from Austria in 1862. The story goes of Mr. Wickenburg's discovery of a promising outcropping of gold quartz, and his later naming the resulting mine "Vulture." The most outstanding mountain peak in the area is also called "Vulture Peak." Henry Wickenburg did not like "hard rock" mining, so he contracted others to do the mining, and he turned his interests toward the cattle business. His ranch was known as "Wickenburg

Ranch," and thus the name of the town when he subsequently gave settlers a portion of his land where the town of Wickenburg now stands. Many people travel through this town daily on their way to someplace else; although, in the winter the town swells in population because of our friends, the winter "snowbirds" from our northern states.

At that time in our lives we began parking our camper in a RV park located diagonally across the street from the Adventist church. This was very convenient for us. We loved our campground hosts, Frank and Beth Board, and we became very good friends. The second winter at their place, we were asked by the Arizona Conference to do a prophecy/evangelistic seminar in Wickenburg. Much to our surprise, but to our delight, Beth and Frank attended this seminar almost every night.

When George got to the presentations concerning end-time prophecies, Beth would go the next day to see her priest at the downtown Catholic Church. Every time that she went to him, he would concur with George as to the facts, etc. We learned of this much later, and it was amusing when you consider that if Beth left the service briefly for any reason, George immediately became concerned that he was offending her. She picked up on this, and regularly left the service to tease George. She was never offended—she later became a baptized member of the Wickenburg Seventh-day Adventist Church. Frank took a little longer to make a decision, but when he did, he called George to come down from Springerville to do the honors of baptism. (That was during our time there before we finally moved to Wickenburg.)

The Lord really blessed that seminar with several baptisms. One couple drove seventy miles roundtrip each night to attend these meetings. The amazing thing about that was that we recorded each presentation and presented it the next night before the scheduled subject. This couple saw all of this series twice because they came early on purpose to see the previous night's subject again. We sincerely appreciated his contribution of expertly installing the latest in sound equipment when we did renovations. It has been an amazing journey for me over the years to see how God works on hearts and lives.

As I said in previous chapters, we realized that we needed a lower elevation because of my health problems. Because of the radiation that I was subjected to in 1987, I developed a blockage in my subclavian artery. A stent was placed; however, that wasn't successful, and I subsequently had a by-pass surgery to allow blood to flow down into my left arm and hand. That surgery was done, and I praise the Lord for His goodness and mercy to me all these days of my life. The doctors were wonderful in their care and skill, and I felt blessed to have them nearby. I have thought that perhaps God allowed these circumstances in our lives to happen so that His Divine purpose could be realized in placing us where He would have us. We fully trust Him in all our ways. We pray His will.

When we took the pastorate in Wickenburg, we and the members realized that the church plant and grounds needed "sprucing up" a bit if we intended to have the public in for evangelism and outreach projects. Again, we and our wonderful members rolled up our sleeves and plunged in for this renovation on the Lord's house. New windows were installed, the balcony was opened up with an additional set of stairs going to that area, the ceilings and chandeliers were cleaned, and the walls were painted. I'm just getting started in telling you about this project: The pews were donated to another church who needed them so badly. We put down new carpet and replaced the pews with pew chairs. (These were less expensive than pews and much more comfortable).

Burger King?

Our conference president at that time, Elder Duane McKey, was always so amused at one of our embellishments. Let me tell you about this: George and I occasionally went to the local Burger King for breakfast. One day when we were there, we noticed that things were changing as far as railings and plants. These rails were made of brass, very pretty and like new. George wanted to place brass rails across the balcony and at the baptistry. We had made a trip to a brass specialty place in Phoenix, and we knew that our little church couldn't afford those high prices. So we went to Burger King and asked what they were going to do with all that brass that they were removing. They were replacing the brass with stainless steel, and they were changing the decorations to desert plants.

The manager called her district supervisor and asked him if our church could have the brass. He said, "Yes!" And we began hauling it to the church to install it around where it was needed. Elder McKey teased George and called it the "Burger King" church. He was really delighted at this wonderful and generous gift from Burger King.

The Man in the Dream

With the church newly renovated and decorated, we launched out for another evangelistic/prophecy crusade. The brochures were printed and scheduled for mailing, and as usual, George went to the local radio station to have our meetings announced for the upcoming weekend opening night As he went into the station, the young woman who was in charge came out from around the desk and exclaimed, "You are the man I saw in my dream! I dreamed that you would be coming in, and that I should attend the meetings that you would be having!" She was so impressed by this set of circumstances that she came to almost all of the meetings, and at the end of the series she was baptized.

> As he went into the station, the young woman who was in charge came out from around the desk and exclaimed, "You are the man I saw in my dream! I dreamed that you would be coming in, and that I should attend the meetings that you would be having!"

You've Found It!

Many times in evangelism the Lord works in ways that simply delights an evangelist and his team. Such was the case when a couple who were long-distance truck drivers showed up at one of our last crusades. Herman and Berdie Gehring came in from a trip one evening, and they were very, very tired and weary from two weeks of driving across country in their big rig truck. Lois, Berdie's mom, had a gourmet supper all prepared for them; they were ready to eat, shower, and catch a few "winks," as the truckers say. But something happened that changed their plans for that evening.

Before coming in home to Congress, Arizona, they had stopped at the post office for their mail. In that stack of mail was a brochure advertising the meetings that were to begin that very night at the Wickenburg Seventh-day Adventist Church. Herman opened the mail and immediately his eyes fell on the colorful brochure which proclaimed that prophecy was going to be featured in these meetings. Since Herman was an ordained minister of another faith, he found himself interested in just what this lecturer was going to be saying.

Herman excitedly exclaimed to Berdie, "Look, Berdie! These meetings seem to be something that we would be interested in. I think we should go down to Wickenburg and see what it's all about."

Berdie didn't feel so excited about leaving home so soon after having just arrived back; nevertheless, she said, "Okay, Herman. Let's go check this out."

When they got to the church, they held on to each other's hand, and Berdie looked at Herman and said, "Let's go, 'Baby-Cakes!'" As they walked in, George came toward them with his out-stretched hand in welcome. He was pleasantly surprised when she said, "We're looking for a church."

Without missing a beat, George replied, "You've found it! Come on in!"

Berdie and Herman told us later how impressed they were with the sweet atmosphere that they felt in the church. George's first presentation was his message on "Unlocking Revelation," and this couple was so impressed with this new information that they canceled plans to immediately go back out on another trip until they could hear more. The wonderful thing to tell you is that since we videotaped each night's presentation that we were able to feed these messages to Berdie's mother, Lois, who also was watching via that medium.

When this couple finally had to leave for another two weeks on the road, George called them by cell phone to check on their Bible studies, and especially on Friday evenings he called to encourage them. He found out that they stopped the truck for the Sabbath hours to observe that sacred time. They were thrilled at all the new truths that they learned through this crusade.

Herman had been baptized by immersion early in his conversion experience; however, Berdie had come from a Mennonite background, and as she said, "They simply poured water over my head and called that baptism." She also revealed that it was quite an eye-opener for her when she found out the biblical way of immersion. Herman chose to be re-baptized, and she was baptized according to the Scriptures. I might say that Lois, who also studied along with the DVDs that she enjoyed, was also baptized with Herman and Berdie.

It was a beautiful thing to witness the power of God displayed in these three decisions. In the ensuing months, Ron and Carrol Halvorsen came to Arizona for the Lay Pastoral Training Seminars held at Camp Yavapines in Prescott, Arizona. This couple completed this training and received their own certificates for services in that area of our church's programs. They were always there to help Ron and Carrol and learn during these training times which greatly aided them in their own walk with the Lord.

The Halvorsens Again!

In 2005, Ron Halvorsen did a prophecy seminar down in Phoenix at the Glendale church. George had promised him that he would assist him with this meeting; however, George made Ron promise that he would come to Wickenburg for a meeting. After George's crusade last time, Ron and Carrol Halvorsen came out to Wickenburg for a ten-day reaping meeting. We were so blessed to have them with us even for such a short time. They were very dear friends, and we could never thank them enough for taking the time from their busy schedule to come to our little church. But they did!

The Piano

Another great blessing and one that I appreciated so much was the addition of a Roland Grand Piano that was donated by Zenna Snowden to our church. (Zenna is now deceased.) This instrument is a marvel, and I could never thank the Lord enough for allowing me, at that time in my life, to be able to play such a fine piano. Two conference musicians came up to present music for George's last crusade. They are wonderful musicians, and we just appreciated them so very much. He played this piano, and remarked that he would like to come up and "just play it for two weeks." I knew what he meant by that remark. The sounds and the touch are unequaled in any other electronic grand.

During our last prophecy seminar, we had a gentleman visitor who remarked that, "I have never seen a church this size that is so electronically advanced." I told you about the latest sound equipment previously, but to that we added, not one, but three fifty-two inch plasma-screen TV monitors that were put in place one on either side of the platform, and one was placed over the back wall of the foyer entrance into the sanctuary. What a blessing! Evangelists now don't have to have spotlights, huge screens, and all that go with that kind of setup. We had theater lights mounted on each side wall and some which shine down from the ceiling. Isn't that wonderful?! I think so when I consider past times when the men would work at setting up far into the night. I remember those days.

George and I were constantly trying to think of ways to uplift the Lord's work and make His message attractive and full of hope. We served an elaborate breakfast each Sabbath morning to any who would enjoy that fellowship and food. We had even put out "the red carpets" for our guests. Everyone said that the Wickenburg church was warm and friendly. We truly hoped that was the impression. Our goal was to lift up the Cross and the Name of Jesus in each Sabbath sermon. It's all about Him, isn't it? We praise His name for the privilege that He gave us to try to be of service to all who came our way. The welcome mat was always out for visitors to that wonderful little corner of Arizona.

Wickenburg, Arizona, is a delightful western town, and the city fathers hold on tight to that image in the atmosphere of the town itself. There are western-theme festivals, ranches, the best museum of western artifacts in the state, roping arenas, rodeos, dude ranches, and western-style shops through downtown. A bypass was built, but I remember the eighteen-wheelers as they used to roll through town as if it was an interstate. I cringed each time that I was at one of the few traffic lights in town when a big rig came rumbling up beside me. We loved this sleepy little town carved out in its niche in time.

We daily tried to think of ways to evangelize in our little corner of Arizona. The CHIP (Complete Health Improvement) program developed by Dr. Hans Diehl was presented by some of our members. This was a great sacrifice of time for some who worked, but it was a good outreach program. Crusades were always planned for springtime and fall when our weather cooperated a little better for good attendance.

We appreciated the emphasis that is placed on evangelism in the Arizona conference. They encouraged pastors to plan at least two evangelistic crusades each year. Arizona is a big supporter of the "Share Him" program sponsored by the Carolina Conference and was directed by Elder Robert Folkenberg and his family. I might say that the present Arizona Conference President, Elder Ed Keyes, and George taught the principles of Share Him Evangelism for two different camp meetings at Camp Yavapines in Prescott, Arizona. We pray that we will do whatever our hands find to do in anticipation of our Lord's return. May He find us all faithful to the end.

Strong Shoulders

Lest I forget, I would be very remiss if I didn't remind you and myself that God's work is built on the efforts of those who came before us. Many are those who sleep and are waiting the return of our Lord and Savior, Jesus Christ. As a people, our continuing endeavors are successful in a large part because these warriors for Christ paid the price of personal sacrifice to spread the gospel far and wide. They endured threats, slights, extreme cold and heat, hardship from lack of personal comfort and convenience. (I heard stories of our pioneers who had to depend on a nearby service station for their needs in that area.) And sometimes their sleeping quarters were cold and inadequate. Some have even stayed in church basements amid the dampness and cold of that place. It is a fact that some prayerfully slept on a cot in a tent somewhere that was pitched on a vacant city lot. As for food, a can of vegetarian beans and crackers was the fare "many a time."

In my small way, I should like to pay tribute to these wonderful predecessors upon whose shoulders our present work is built. I think of Elder E. E. Cleveland, who was instrumental in the work in my city at that time in Winston-Salem, North Carolina. The Richards, Fagals, Vandemans, Bradfords, Cemers, and others that you know. Our current evangelists are also carrying on the work of evangelism begun long centuries ago. I say, "Thank you, Father, for their lives and devotion to Your cause." May we never forget!

These days there is a lot of church planting going on with very good results. May we all stand by these dear ones as they endeavor to bring the good news of the gospel to these new places. Recently, George and I were traveling down a country road, and we commented that perhaps the people there had never seen nor heard of a Seventh-day Adventist Church. Someone must tell them about Jesus and the other truths that are found in God's Holy Word. Will you?

Isaiah 30:17: "till ye be left as a beacon upon the top of a mountain, and as an ensign upon a hill."

Chapter Twelve

The List

In these twilight years, I feel a sense of real contentment as far as my day-to-day living. George is a wonderful, caring husband—I couldn't ask for anything more. Over the years he has proven his love for me, and at the same time, he has proven his own self-worth. He has worked long and hard, and no one could ever call him lazy. He is diligent in the Lord's service, and I greatly admire his tenacity in all his endeavors. He loves the Lord with all his heart.

There are times when the two of us briefly look back, and we look forward as far as we dare; then it is that we wish that we had another set of time to once again give to God. We remark on occasion that the two of us have traveled many miles together—we went to the other side of the world clasping each other's hand, and, at the same time, holding on to God's hand with the other one. For the two of us, evangelism was and still is a passion. We can't "retire." There are too many places to go and too many things to see, for it is in the context of Matthew 28:18–20 that I say these things:

Jesus said, "**Go** ye therefore, and teach all nations, baptizing them in the name of the Father, and of the Son, and of the Holy Ghost: Teaching them to observe all things whatsoever I have commanded you:" And His very last words, "And lo, I am with you always, even unto the end of the world," have accompanied us wherever we have gone. We have clung to these words when flying over the Atlantic Ocean to Moscow and Moldova; we have clung to them on opening nights of crusades when we didn't know who would show up. These comforting

> *There are times when the two of us briefly look back, and we look forward as far as we dare; then it is that we wish that we had another set of time to once again give to God*

words have gone with us into the operating rooms when we were at our weakest moments. How can we help loving this wonderful Lord!

The things to **see** are the souls who have come to the foot of the cross in surrender to Jesus with a commitment to follow Him in complete obedience to His will. The many other things to see are His faithful saints who will commit to discipleship and to the task of training others. It is members who are able who will "pitch in" to help raise up a church and help build or renovate an existing structure. It is a beautiful thing to witness when there is harmony and purpose among the followers of Jesus.

As I mentioned earlier, from our beginning in evangelism, George and I considered ourselves freelancers. There was an element of freedom in that frame of mind that allowed us to go wherever we felt led to go without thought of financial rewards. We sincerely wanted to fit into any place or role that God would place on us.

On June 9, 2007, the Arizona Conference of Seventh-day Adventists bestowed on George the honor of ordination for the sacred work of the gospel ministry. This ceremony of ordination was witnessed at the annual camp meeting at Camp Yavapines in Prescott, Arizona. George received this in a spirit of humility and with the knowledge that his calling was affirmed by his respected peers. You might say that it was a wonderful and joyous experience for us.

George and I went through health challenges as adults. But when I think of my siblings, perhaps my medical history was the worst; then, again, God always sees us through these periods of time. As I come to the close of my words to you, please let me give God praise for a glorious event in my young life. It seemed to have set the stage for my path in living. It surely was an affirmation of my faith in my God that would sustain me as I traveled down my road of life.

In my earliest childhood, I endured ear infections that would be no problem now with antibiotics available at any pharmacy with a doctor's prescription. My parents took me to several doctors without any promise for my cure. The pain in my ears was excruciating, and at times I would cry uncontrollably from it. Walking the floor at night with pain was common for one so young as I.

One night after a very moving revival meeting at my childhood church, I told my mother that I wanted "Preacher Campbell" to pray for my ears to be healed. Mom stopped him in the aisle on our way out of church and relayed my request to him. He put his hand on my head and prayed a very simple prayer for my healing. In faith I believed that God would heal me, and He did! Since that time I have endeavored to maintain a trust in my Heavenly Father, and He is ever by my side. Praise His Name!

I praise God for His loving care over my life. I thank Him for extending His mercy to me in the forgiveness of my sins and giving me the promise of eternal life. I give Him praise for the knowledge of the Sabbath and the other truths that we hold so very dear. (Suppose Mom had refused to buy those books from the colporteurs of long ago? Suppose! Suppose!)

Today as I sat out on the porch enjoying His wonderful creation, I asked Him once again to please let me be there when He makes all things new. I'm also looking forward to that new body when all pain is gone for me and for you, too. I find that I ask myself more and more these questions: "Are you really prepared for eternity? Have you done the will of God?" These are sobering questions with which all must come to terms. Our salvation has been paid for by Jesus' sacrificial death on the cross, and our decisions must be made to follow Jesus daily in a total surrender to Him and His will for our lives. It is a walk by faith, isn't it? Romans 10:17, 18 tells us, "So then faith cometh by hearing and hearing by the word of God. But I say, Have they not heard? Yes, verily, Their sound went into all the earth, and their words unto the ends of the world."

The Book of Ephesians contains the whole list as I see it. He chose us from the foundation of the world, and it is up to us to choose Him. In Him we have redemption through His blood and the forgiveness of sins according to the riches of His grace. We once were dead in trespasses and sins, and we once walked according to the way of this world, but now by grace we have been saved, and it should be our delight to do His will. We are part of His church, His body of believers as a holy temple in the Lord.

The list includes all people, and it is our duty to see that the Good News of the Gospel reaches all people, and that we walk in unity. Paul admonishes us to:

1. Walk worthy of the calling with which we were called.
2. Walk in lowliness, gentleness, long suffering, and bearing each other's burdens.
3. Always remember that there is one Lord, one faith, one baptism, one God and Father of all.
4. Remember that some are apostles, some prophets, some evangelists, some pastors, and some teachers and this is for the equipping of the saints for the work of ministry.
5. We are to speak the truth in love as Christ Jesus would.
6. We are to put off our former conduct and put on the new man that was created according to God in righteousness and true holiness. A life of obedience to His commands.

Chapter four and verses 23–31 give us things on the list that we shouldn't do. It ends in verse 32 by saying; "And be ye kind one to another, tenderhearted, forgiving one another, even as God for Christ's sake hath forgiven you."

The two remaining chapters tell us how to continue our walk of obedience toward the coming of Jesus. It is profound, and we would do well to include Ephesians often in our Bible readings. I also like what is revealed in James 1:27: "Pure religion and undefiled before God and the Father is this, To visit the fatherless and widows in their affliction, and to keep himself unspotted from the world."

I like the little section in the book, *Evangelism* by Ellen G. White, titled "Evangelism Our Real Work." "Evangelistic work, opening the Scriptures to others, warning men and women of what is coming upon the world, is to occupy more and still more of the time of God's servants" (*Review and Herald*, August 2, 1906, p. 17). George soon will be eighty, and he says that he can't ever completely retire. There are still those out there who haven't yet heard. I would say that he is forever committed to being an evangelist no matter in the way that it happens: pastor, evangelist, teacher, or that good neighbor down the street who stands ready to help as long as God gives him strength.

Jude, verse 24, 25: "Now unto him that is able to keep you from falling, and to present you faultless before the presence of his glory with exceeding joy. To the only wise God our Savior, be glory, and majesty, dominion and power, both now and ever. A-men."

May you, my dear reader, walk with me as we continue our journey toward the Kingdom. Jesus is looking back at us and motioning for us to follow Him closely, ever so closely on this shining pathway that ends at the STREETS OF GOLD.

EPILOGUE

Every story has to come to a conclusion, but not without the knowledge that life continues on for the storyteller after the conclusion. Toward the end of our time in Arizona, our youngest daughter, Lorie, was diagnosed with small-cell carcinoma of the lungs. We felt that perhaps we should retire and go back to North Carolina to be of assistance to her. At the same time, my elderly brothers and wives weren't doing so well health wise, and we knew that they needed some help.

With the help of some friends, we did an outreach program in the little community of Hudson, North Carolina. Elder Ron Halvorsen did his last crusade in Charlotte, North Carolina, and he asked George if he would help him with that. We moved into a furnished, rental house for that meeting, and I only went to one or two meetings because of health issues. But, Elder Halvorsen had a beautiful baritone voice, and he teased the audience in Charlotte that he was going to sing on the very last night of the meeting. Ron's one and only song was "The Wonder of It All." If you didn't see Ron singing and only heard him, you would have thought that it was George Beverly Shea singing.

Ron had been accustomed to my accompanying him when he sang this song, so he insisted that I come and play for him to sing on that very last night. Because of my problem with balance, George led me out on stage to the piano, and when I played an introduction for him, the audience gasped, and you could hear them say, "He really is going to sing." When he finished singing, the crowd spontaneously stood to their feet and started clapping, praising the Lord, and saying good things. George and I quietly walked to the back of the curtain.

Ron was ill even during this last meeting, but as his custom was, he proved faithful to the end of the crusade. After that it was to be first one thing and another, and in the end he peacefully fell asleep to wait for the coming of the Life-Giver, our Blessed Lord and Savior, Jesus Christ. He and Carrol forever blessed our lives. Carrol was a true and faithful wife as she was ever by Ron's side.

Bill and Cora "Sunshine" Waters reside in Apopka, Florida, where she is recuperating from some health issues. Again, I will say that Sunshine was always by Bill's side to help him. She was dedicated to this work, and she was a very creative person in making the different halls look nice. We'll always appreciate their "hovering over us" when we first began our time in public evangelism. They were truly there for us if we needed their love and wisdom.

Dr. Harmon Brownlow passed away some few years back, and his wife, Margaret, lives in Florida. In the summer she enjoys her North Carolina mountain home above the town of Lansing. Early on, Margaret kept the "home fires burning" in the care of their children while Harmon was away in evangelism weeks at a time. Such a sacrifice for them. And I might say that before her retirement she taught school at Forest Lake Academy until the children were grown. It was then that she joined Dr. Brownlow in their travels and in their passion for evangelism.

George now does an occasional crusade with his last one held in Kannapolis, North Carolina. We lost our Lorie in January 2019, and we greatly miss that dear, sweet girl. My brothers and their wives are now deceased, and I miss them, too. I only have one sister left from our large family of long ago. I live each day in anticipation of the return of Jesus. George is mostly retired; yet, he still wants to be involved in evangelism as long as he is able. We enjoy our local church with its happy and busy members.

At this point, we have several family members who don't seem to be so concerned about their own soul salvation, and we pray for them. When I'm out and about, I still scan the skies in anticipation of Jesus' return. With the world conditions as they are at the present time, it pays all of us to heed Jesus' words when He said, "Watch therefore: for ye know not what hour your Lord doth come."

TEACH Services, Inc.
PUBLISHING

We invite you to view the complete
selection of titles we publish at:
www.TEACHServices.com

We encourage you to write us
with your thoughts about this,
or any other book we publish at:
info@TEACHServices.com

TEACH Services' titles may be purchased in
bulk quantities for educational, fund-raising,
business, or promotional use.
bulksales@TEACHServices.com

Finally, if you are interested in seeing
your own book in print, please contact us at:
publishing@TEACHServices.com
We are happy to review your manuscript at no charge.

www.ingramcontent.com/pod-product-compliance
Lightning Source LLC
Chambersburg PA
CBHW070543170426
43200CB00011B/2538